The Philatelic History of Diabetes

IN SEARCH OF A CURE

Lee J. Sanders, DPM

American Diabetes Association.

Director, Book Publishing, John Fedor; *Associate Director, Professional Books, and Editor,* Christine B. Welch; *Production Manager,* Peggy M. Rote; *Composition,* Circle Graphics, Inc.; *Cover Design,* Kathy Tresnak, Koncept, Inc.; *Printer,* Transcontinental Printing Inc.

Printed in Canda
1 3 5 7 9 10 8 6 4 2

Reasonable steps have been taken to ensure the accuracy of the information presented. The American Diabetes Association—its officers, directors, employees, volunteers, and members—assumes no responsibility or liability for personal or other injury, loss, or damage that may result from the suggestions or information in this publication.

⊗ The paper in this publication meets the requirements of the ANSI Standard Z39.48-1992 (permanence of paper).

ADA titles may be purchased for business or promotional use or for special sales. For information, please write to Lee Romano Sequeira, Special Sales & Promotions, at the address below.

American Diabetes Association
1701 North Beauregard Street
Alexandria, Virginia 22311

Library of Congress Cataloging-in-Publication Data

Sanders, Lee J., 1947-
   The philatelic history of diabetes : in search of a cure / Lee J. Sanders.
      p. cm.
   Includes bibliographical references.
   ISBN 1-58040-126-0 (alk. paper) —ISBN 1-58040-084-1 (pbk. : alk. paper)
   1. Physicians on postage stamps. 2. Postage stamps. 3. Diabetes—History.   I. Title.
 HE6182.P5 S36 2001
 769.56'49362196462—dc21
                                2001033533

To my wife Debra—
the compass in my life,
and to my children Lauren, Douglas, and Rebecca—
the pride and joy in my life.

Contents

Foreword

The transmission of information over long distances goes back to remote antiquity. The Greek historian Herodotus wrote about the postal system of the Persians BCE.[1] The prepaid adhesive label that we know as the postage stamp is of much later vintage, the first being issued in Great Britain on May 1, 1840, called the Penny Black. Early stamps showed either the commercial value or an effigy of the ruler.

Since then, the number of stamp-issuing countries and stamps issued has grown remarkably. According to the Universal Postal Union, there were 189 stamp-issuing countries and some territories with independent stamp-issuing privileges in 1996.[2] In 1997, 1,100 million items were posted each day in post offices or letter boxes for delivery within national borders. In the same year, about 24 million posted items crossed international frontiers. In 1998, 14,597 postage stamps and souvenir sheets were issued by 246 countries (20 stamp-issuing countries did not issue any new

---

[1] Herodotus (?484–420 BCE) was describing the expedition of the Greeks against the Persians under Cyrus, around 539 BCE. The Chinese and Egyptians had 'postal' systems much earlier.

[2] Postal statistics. Available from *http://www.upu.org*.

stamps that year.) Forty-two countries, including Australia, Canada, South Africa, and the United States, issued more than 100 stamps that year.[3]

Stamps, and other philatelic material, represent a country's past, present, and future; its geography and history; its beliefs, pride, shame, and concerns. The first stamp commemorating an event or a person was issued by New South Wales in 1888. Stamps are ubiquitous, small, colorful, inexpensive, and useful. Each stamp is seen by at least two people, the sender and the recipient, and often by many more. It is thus surprising that the informative and instructional content of stamps has been so persistently ignored.

In 1929, Dr. Fielding H. Garrison, doyen of medical history, remarked that stamps were a great resource for medical historians, something he hoped that physicians would soon recognize.[4] His prediction has hardly come to fruition in the years since then, even though there are a number of dedicated medical philatelists and five journals devoted exclusively to medical philately—two are English, one German, one Japanese, and one Romanian. Medical philatelic articles are frequently seen in the philatelic press but are rare in the medical press.

As a confirmed and vocal believer in the educational aspects of stamps, I am excited by Dr. Sanders' expert utilization of applicable stamps to illustrate and annotate the struggle against diabetes. As a life-threatening disease, diabetes has been recognized for centuries. According to the National Institute of Diabetes and Digestive and Kidney Disease, 15.7 million people (5.9 percent of the population) in the United States have diabetes— 10.3 million are diagnosed, and 5.4 million are undiagnosed.[5] The

---

[3] McCarty D: Stamps of 1998 total new record of 14,597. *Linn's Stamp News* January 24, 2000, p. 32.

[4] Garrison FH: A brief note on medical philately. *Annals of Medical History, New Series* 1:451–52, 1929.

[5] Prevalence of diabetes. Available from http://www.niddk.nih.gov/ health/diabetes/pubs/dmstats/dmstats.htm#prev. Accessed 29 March 2001.

disease seems to be increasing rapidly in this country. The life-endangering implications of diabetes worldwide are clearly stupendous. The progressive effects of unrecognized and untreated diabetes are particularly malignant, as they generally manifest during the productive years, the mortality among middle-aged people with diabetes being approximately twice that of a comparable population without diabetes.

Most of us are aware of the dangers of diabetes, yet the history of its recognition and attempted control is largely ignored. This is disappointing. We stand on the shoulders of giants, and it is but proper that we should pay homage to those who have led the way.[6] Dr. Sanders has done a great service by clearly yet succinctly describing how our knowledge of the disease, its ravages, and its control has evolved and identifying the fascinating individuals involved.

Although a recent booklet on diabetes is nicely illustrated and has a reasonable coverage of the philatelic representation of diabetes,[7] Dr. Sanders' book is the first full account of the history, search for cure, and philatelic associations of its kind. The depth and width of his coverage will be a boon to philatelists, especially medical philatelists. I hope that this well-written and beautifully illustrated book will bring the charm and the informational content of stamps to many. I commend Dr. Sanders for his effort and expertise in writing the book and the American Diabetes Association for its wisdom in making its publication possible.

RANÈS C. CHAKRAVORTY
Distinguished Topical Philatelist—
American Topical Association, 1992
Editor & Publisher, *Scalpel & Tongs*,
The American Journal of Medical Philately

---

[6] The Sanskrit epic Mahabharata in a famous verse states that "the path to be followed is that trodden by the Great" (Mah_janassah gata jena sa panth_).

[7] Shafrir E: *History and Perspective of Diabetes Illustrated by Postage Stamps*. London, Tel Aviv, Freund Publishing House, 1999.

Foreword

In 1971, the Canadian government issued a 6¢ postage stamp commemorating the 50th anniversary of the isolation of insulin by Banting and Best. That year, Stuart Soeldner at the Joslin Diabetes Center used the stamp in an article in *Diabetes Forecast* to illustrate the size of the implantable glucose sensor platinum electrode that he and his colleagues were developing. I made a slide of that *Forecast* illustration. I use it now to indicate the unpredictably slow progress of scientific research, as 30 years passed until we witnessed the first implantation in a human of a continuous glucose sensor last year—not the platinum electrode of the 1970s, but an intravascular sensor developed by MiniMed and an affiliated company, MRG. That stamp hangs on my wall in a plaque along with four other stamps also commemorating aspects of the history of diabetes.

Thus, I was aware that stamps had been used to illuminate diabetes history. I was not surprised then when, during a break at a meeting we were attending, Dr. Lee Sanders mentioned that he had compiled a historical perspective on diabetes through a special collection of stamps. I was so intrigued by his collection that I asked the meeting organizers to invite Lee to present his collection at our next meeting, which he did. And

I was captivated. Lee had collected dozens of stamps that had been issued in various parts of the world, each illustrating some aspect of medical history that could be related to diabetes. Equally important, Lee had carefully researched the historical aspects of the subjects depicted on the stamps. In doing so, he created a fascinating account that readers will find most intriguing—an exciting history of one of the most important diseases to afflict humankind.

Now, he has shared that collection with us, with royalties donated to the American Diabetes Association Research Foundation—another testimony to the special nature of Dr. Lee Sanders. The photos of the stamps in this book are a joy to behold and make a stamp enthusiast such as myself proud. I was truly honored to be asked to write this foreword and hope that you find this collection as interesting and exciting as I did.

Jay S. Skyler, MD
University of Miami

Preface

Regrettably, health care providers today receive very little instruction in the history of medicine. Most medical and nursing students have a limited, contemporary knowledge of diabetes. The history of advances in diabetes before the discovery of insulin in 1921 has been obscured by the passage of time. Historical concepts of the causes and nature of diabetes have either been forgotten or never learned. Yet, knowing the history of diabetes gives us a better understanding of the issues and clearer vision as we look to the future. Therefore, my challenge and passion is to share this thrilling story and to reveal the origin of many of the terms used when talking about this disease: diabetes mellitus, pancreas, islet cells, insulin, glycogen, isletin, C-peptide, and radioimmunoassay.

The reader should understand that a philatelic version of the history of any aspect of medicine cannot be totally comprehensive. I have attempted to highlight major milestones in the evolution of our understanding of diabetes. The omission of any event or individual's role in the history of diabetes in no way lessens the importance of that contribution.

I wish to acknowledge the invaluable research assistance provided by Barbara Deaven, medical librarian, and Dorothy Melan, library technician, VA Medical Center, Lebanon, Pennsylvania; Miriam Mandelbaum, curator, and Arlene Shaner, reference librarian, Malloch Rare Book Room, The New York Academy of Medicine; and Lynne Dent, library assistant, Glasgow University Library.

The story of diabetes is an exciting chronicle of descriptive clinical observations, diagnostic tests, experimental research, therapeutic advances, and disabling complications. I trust that you will enjoy reading this narrative and experience genuine optimism as we search for a cure in the 21st century.

Introduction

The story of diabetes mellitus—its discovery, description, and treatment—is a remarkable narrative covering 3,500 years of medical history. This story is still being written. Until we find a cure, thousands of scientists and clinicians will continue to work to unravel the medical mystery of diabetes and to care for the more than 150 million people worldwide affected by this disease.

I have chosen to convey a concise history of diabetes, in a rather novel way, illustrated with postage stamps from around the world. Late in life, I discovered the thrill of stamp collecting, known as philately, through an article that appeared December 1994 in *Diabetes Forecast*,[1] the members' magazine of the American Diabetes Association.

In his article "Stamping Out Diabetes," philatelist Raymond Schuessler, who has diabetes, introduced me to the beauty and historical value of postage stamps. Schuessler's collection of stamps related to diabetes made his historical essay on diabetes intriguing. I immediately knew that I coveted the stamps and had to acquire my own collection. I could visualize how lovely the set would look framed and hanging on the wall over my desk. The only problem was that I didn't know how to go about finding the stamps. So began the experience that has led me to write this book.

With a copy of the *Forecast* article in hand, I contacted local stamp dealer Bill Levengood. He explained to me how stamps are cataloged and suggested that I locate a copy of the Scott Stamp Catalog. I quickly found a well-worn 1985 4-volume set in the patient library of the Lebanon VA (Veterans Affairs) Medical Center, where I see patients. Bill's second bit of advice was to join a thematic stamp association, through which I could locate other philatelists with similar collecting interests. I soon became a member of the American Topical Association (ATA) and ATA's Medical Subjects Unit. My membership included two very helpful journals, which are worthy of note: *Topical Time*, ATA's *Journal of Thematic Philately*, and the *American Journal of Medical Philately, Scalpel & Tongs*.

I was now ready to surf the Internet and locate my stamps. This marked the beginning of an exciting and challenging hobby. The collection and study of postage stamps, postmarks, and postal materials related to medicine is termed medical philately. Philately provides a stimulating pictorial history of medicine and clinical research. Medical philately has taken me via the Internet around the world and introduced me to many new friends and a wealth of knowledge about the history of medicine.

Until 2001, the United States had not issued a stamp for diabetes or a commemorative stamp for the discovery of insulin. This was puzzling to me, because so many other countries, large and small, some far less affected by the toll of diabetes than the United States, had issued stamps related to diabetes. Thanks to the efforts of the United States Postal Service, the first-class postage stamp "Know More About Diabetes" is now raising diabetes awareness in our country.

Periods in
Diabetes History

Medical historians have previously divided the history of diabetes into four periods, each characterized by advancing medical knowledge and scientific inquiry.[2,3] These phases are:

- The Descriptive Period: describing and naming the disease
- The Diagnostic Period: learning how to diagnose the disease
- The Experimental Period: learning what causes the disease
- The Therapeutic Era: learning how to treat the disease

In addition to using these divisions in this book, I have added a fifth period, the Era of Complications, in which we learn how diabetes causes additional health problems. Without question, periods overlap: the Experimental Period and the Therapeutic Era are advancing simultaneously. These periods, along with their prominent figures, seminal discoveries, controversies, and complications, are illustrated by postage stamps from 30 different countries.

As we proceed through these evolutionary periods, the modern reader will appreciate the changes in views regarding the cause of this disease, from the kidneys and bladder, to the stomach, and finally to the pancreas. Approaches to the treatment of diabetes unfold gradually, as physicians begin to understand the nature of this ailment. At first, we see a variety of unsavory dietary approaches to treatment, including starvation diets, and then in the early 20th century, there is the miraculous discovery of insulin. Diabetes monitoring begins with primitive taste tests of the urine for "sweetness," and progresses to the development of more sensitive qualitative and quantitative tests for urine and blood glucose. In the 1970s, we see the beginning of a revolution in diabetes care: self-monitoring of blood glucose.

Looking at diabetes throughout history makes one fact clear: The incidence of diabetes has increased dramatically, from an uncommon ailment during the period of antiquity to a worldwide epidemic expected to affect 300 million people by the year 2025.

The
Descriptive
Period

THE AGE OF ANTIQUITY

The story of diabetes unfolds during the Age of Antiquity, where we begin to see the earliest descriptions of the symptoms of diabetes. Ancient physicians recorded their observations in an attempt to better understand the nature of the ailment, its origin, and treatment.

It is commonly believed that the history of medicine began with the Greeks, and that before the time of Hippocrates there was little that could be called an "art of medicine." Nevertheless, for more than 2,000 years before the birth of the Greek physician Hippocrates, Egyptian physicians had been striving to diagnose and treat disease.

Two notable Egyptian physicians, **Imhotep** and **Thoth**, were elevated to the position of gods in the Egyptian Pantheon. Imhotep was revered as the God of Medicine and has been described as "the first figure of a physician to stand out clearly from the mists of antiquity."[4-6] Thoth was known as the God of the Healing Art, patron god of physicians.

Figure 1 shows a stamp commemorating the 100th Anniversary of the Medical Department of Cairo University and the International Medical Congress. The illustration of Imhotep was taken from a wall picture in the remains of the Temple of

FIGURE 1
Egypt 1928, Sc#153. Imhotep, 100th Anniversary of the Medical Department, University of Cairo.

Imhotep, at Philae Island.[6] Imhotep is shown seated, holding an ankh, the Egyptian symbol of life, in his left hand. In his right hand is a staff that symbolizes his reign. Imotep is also featured on stamps issued by Egypt in 1968 and 1981. (Refer to the Philatelic Checklist at the end of this book.) Egyptian medicine influenced the medical practices of adjoining cultures, including the culture of ancient Greece.

Egyptian Medicine

Ancient Egypt was the first civilization known to have a wide-ranging study of medicine and to have surviving written records of its practices and procedures. Among the oldest existing medical writings are seven papyri from the period between 2000 and 1200 BCE.* The Kahun, Smith, Ebers, Hearst, London, Berlin, and Chester Beatty papyri describe the ancient practice of Egyptian medicine.

The first reference to diabetes mellitus is attributed to the most famous of these papyri, the Ebers Papyrus, which was written about 1550 BCE and acquired by German Egyptologist Georg Ebers while excavating in the vicinity of Thebes in 1872. Among the collection of 811 prescriptions for specified disorders in this papyrus, along with magical spells and incantations, are remedies for the treatment of excessive urination, called polyuria.[7] Polyuria is a hallmark of untreated diabetes.

---

*BCE is an acronym for "Before the Common Era" and is equivalent to BC.

Paragraph 264 of the Ebers Papyrus provides the following remedy "to eliminate urine which is too plentiful," although it is uncertain whether the condition described was increased amount or increased frequency of urination:

> A measuring glass filled with
>> Water from the bird pond
>> Elderberry
>> Fibres of the asit plant
>> Fresh milk
>> Beer-swill
>> Flower of the cucumber
>> Green dates
>
> Make into one, strain, and take for four days.

Figure 2 shows a commemorative stamp issued in 1971 by Egypt for the World Health Organization's World Health Day. The stamp features a section of the Ebers Papyrus, mentioning polyuria, and a portrait of the famous Egyptian physician

FIGURE 2
Egypt 1971, Sc#864.
Ebers Papyrus, Hesy Re, and WHO emblem.

Hesy Re. Hesy Re was chief of dentists and physicians to the pyramid builders of the third dynasty, around 2600 BCE. He is shown wearing a scribe's palette and reed holder.

The Ebers Papyrus, reportedly the largest, most beautiful, and best preserved of the medical papyri, is preserved at the University of Leipzig, Germany. The German Democratic Republic also issued a stamp featuring the Ebers Papyrus in 1991. (Refer to the Philatelic Checklist at the end of this book.)

Greek Medicine

Hippocrates (460–377 BCE) was a Greek physician regarded as the "father of medicine." He became the most renowned physician of the period of antiquity. According to Osler, "What Socrates did for philosophy, Hippocrates may be said to have done for medicine . . . Hippocrates insisted upon the practical nature of the art (of medicine) and in placing its highest good in the benefit of the patient."[4] For 2,500 years, his name has been associated with the famous Hippocratic oath, in which physicians promise to do their patients no harm.

One of the greatest contributions to medicine by Hippocrates and his school is the art of accurate observation.[4] His observations of the sick led him to teach that diseases were a natural process, not divine or sacred. The physician's charge was to assist nature in reestablishing a patient's health. Hippocrates himself did not specifically mention diabetes; however,

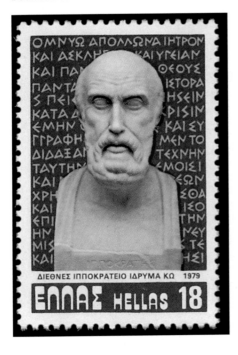

FIGURE 3
Greece 1979, Sc#1326. Statue of Hippocrates and his oath, memorial stamp for the Hippocratic Foundation.

there are accounts in the *Hippocratic* writings that are consistent with the signs and symptoms of diabetes. There are references to excessive urinary flow with wasting of the body.[8,9] In *Epidemics, Book III*, "the amount of urine passed was great; it was not proportional to the amount drunk but considerably in excess . . . the urine which was passed was also markedly bad . . . in most cases these signs signified some wasting."[9]

To this day, Hippocrates represents the ethical ideal of a compassionate, dedicated, selfless physician. Figure 3 shows a sculpture of Hippocrates with his oath in the background. This is a memorial stamp for the Hippocratic Foundation issued by Greece in 1979. Hippocrates is also featured on stamps issued by Australia, Hungary, Yemen, and Syria. (Refer to the Philatelic Checklist at the end of this book.)

Hippocrates, in *Regimen in Acute Diseases*, written in 400 BCE, promoted the concept of preventive medicine. He stressed the influence of diet, exercise, and lifestyle on health. "A change in regimen may have considerable beneficial affects . . . it is also important that the diet administered after the change should be correct." There is also a caution against fad diets. "It is well known that a low diet of food and drink is on the whole a surer way to health than violent changes from one diet to another."[9] Healthy, active lifestyle and moderation in eating are cornerstones of diabetes treatment today.

Claudius Galen (130–201 CE*) was a Greek physician, a brilliant scholar, and the most influential medical writer of all time. For more than 1,500 years, his extensive works were the irreproachable authority on medicine. Galen had a dominating influence on the development of Arabian and European medical practice. Not until the Renaissance did physicians begin to question the infallibility of his writings. Galen attended the best medical schools, including Alexandria, the first great medical school of antiquity. He is considered the greatest name in Greek medicine after Hippocrates.

---

*CE is an acronym for "Common Era" and is equivalent to AD.

FIGURE 4
Hungary 1989,
Sc#3213. Galen
130–201 CE.

Galen discussed diabetes in a number of his works and described the condition as rare. He referred to the ailment as dropsy into the pot, diarrhea of the urine, the thirsty disease, and the strong thirst.[8,10,11] He incorrectly noted that its site of action was in the kidneys. In his work *On the Localization of Diseases*, Galen wrote, "I am of the opinion that the kidneys are affected in the rare disease which some people call chamberpot dropsy, other again diabetes or violent thirst. For my own part I have seen the disease till now only twice when the patients suffered from an inextinguishable thirst, which forced them to drink enormous quantities; the fluid was urinated swiftly with a urine resembling the drink." [10]

Although Galen excelled in comparative anatomy, his anatomical studies were performed primarily on lower animals, particularly apes and pigs, which led to errors in his treatises on human anatomy. He believed that the pancreas served as a protective cushion for the stomach, as well as the adjacent blood vessels. He also observed that the pancreas was the source of a secreted fluid of unknown function. Galen's portrait is depicted on stamps issued by Hungary in 1989 (Figure 4) and by Yemen in 1966. The stamp from Yemen commemorates completion of the World Health Organization's new headquarters building.

Aretaeus (130–200 CE) was a disciple of Hippocrates and a contemporary of Galen, from the Roman province of Cappadocia, in Asia Minor. He provided the first accurate description of the symptoms of diabetes and was the first to use the term *diabetes* in connection with this condition.[10,12–14] As you will see, Aretaeus employed the word *diabetes* from the Greek word that denotes a *siphon*. Both Aretaeus and Galen emphasized the rarity of this ailment and its symptoms of excessive thirst and frequent urination. Aretaeus' classic description of diabetes appears in his treatise *On The Causes And Symptoms Of Chronic Diseases, Book II*. The following is a translation of his writings by Francis Adams.[14] Some portions are omitted.

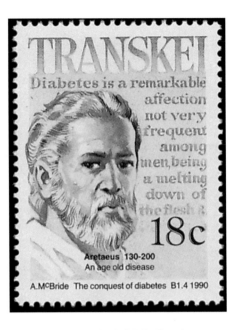

FIGURE 5
Transkei 1990, Sc#235. Aretaeus 130–200, An Age Old Disease. The conquest of diabetes B1.4.

"DIABETES is a wonderful affection, not very frequent among men, being a melting down of the flesh and limbs into urine. . . . The course is the common one, namely, the kidneys and bladder; for the patients never stop making water, but the flow is incessant, as if from the opening of the aqueducts. The nature of the disease, then, is chronic, and it takes a long period to form; but the patient is short-lived, if the constitution of the disease be completely established; for the melting is rapid, the death speedy. Moreover, life is disgusting and painful; thirst, unquenchable; excessive drinking, which, however, is disproportionate to the large quantity of urine, for more urine is passed; and one cannot stop them either from drinking or making water . . . Hence, the disease appears to me to have got the name of *diabetes*, as if from the Greek word which signifies a siphon, because the fluid does not remain in the body, but uses the man's body as a ladder, whereby to leave it."[14]

Figure 5 shows a stamp issued by Transkei in 1990 featuring the image of Aretaeus and a brief section of his description of diabetes. This is the first of four stamps in a commemorative titled The Conquest of Diabetes. Transkei was one of South Africa's Bantu homelands, a semiautonomous state for disenfranchised black South Africans, which existed for only a brief period from 1976 to 1994.

The term *pancreas* is derived from the Greek words for *all flesh* (pan = all, kreas = flesh) because of the organ's seeming lack of supporting structure. The origin of the term is not known for certain. Papaspyros notes that Herophilus of Chalcedon (c. 270 BCE) first described the pancreas.[2] Others have attributed this to the Greek physician and anatomist Rufus of Ephesus (c. 100 CE). Rufus trained at the first great medical school of antiquity in Alexandria, Egypt, and was renowned for his investigations of the heart and eye. In his treatise *Medical Questions*, Rufus advocated questioning the patient to better recognize the nature of his illness and to provide better treatment. This is the first Greek medical treatise that discusses the art of medical history taking.[15]

Hindu Medicine

Hindu physicians are credited with coining the term *honey urine* a millennium before the first Europeans added *mellitus*, meaning honey, to the term *diabetes*. Ayurvedic medicine, ancient Indian medical tradition, can be traced back to the old Vedic Scriptures (veda meaning knowledge) written in Sanskrit. Much later on, this knowledge was compiled into three medical textbooks called *samhitas*, named for three legendary Hindu physicians, **Charaka**, **Susruta**, and **Vagbhata**, collectively called the Holy Triad. The original texts of these physicians were not preserved, so we cannot be certain who they were and exactly when they lived, but it is believed that their samhitas originated between 100 BCE and 700 CE.[16]

Charaka and Vagbhata described 20 different varieties of prameha, or "diseased flow of urine," classified according to the qualities of the urine, such as color, odor, and sediment. Charaka observed that in certain types of diseased flow of urine, "the patient gradually loses strength, flesh and healthy glow of complexion."[16] Advanced cases were complicated with abscesses, carbuncles, bad smelling breath (acidosis), and even loss of consciousness.

The Hindus used the terms *iksumeha* (sugar cane urine) and *madhumeha* (honey urine). These terms apparently compared the color of the urine to the juice of the sugar cane or honey. Charaka and Susruta mentioned the attraction of insects (ants and flies) to the urine of people afflicted with iksumeha. Contrary to popular belief, the samhitas do not mention anyone actually tasting urine with the tongue.[16]

Hindu physicians observed that prameha could be inherited or acquired. Vagbhata mentioned diabetes acquired as a result of obesity: "An idle man who indulges in day-sleep or follows sedentary pursuits or is in the habit of taking sweet liquids or fat-making food, will ere long fall an easy victim of the disease." The following signs and symptoms were observed to be associated with prameha: excessive thirst, frequent and copious urination, obesity, fatigue, impotence, and infections.

Treatment was based on observation of the symptoms and consisted of the generous administration of purgatives and emetics, as well as a diet rich in carbohydrates with added honey. It appears that the ancient Hindu physicians failed to make the connection between a carbohydrate-rich diet and the observation of honey urine or sugar cane

FIGURE 6
Nepal 1977, Sc#337. Dhanvantari, Health Day.

urine. However, weight reduction and physical exercise were appropriately recommended. Vagbhata emphasized the importance of prevention. "It is necessary to prevent any inflammation in diabetes with greatest care. For as soon as inflammation has taken place, its improvement and cure depends upon the will of the Gods."[16]

Dhanvantari was a minor Hindu deity who served as physician for other gods and was regarded as the Divine Healer. In Figure 6, he is shown in his four-armed form holding the wheel and conch in the upper right and left hands. In the other two hands, there are a nectar pot and an herb. Nepal issued this stamp to commemorate Health Day in Nepal, November 9, 1977.

Chinese Medicine

The *Nei Ching*, or *Canon of Internal Medicine*, is the basis of Chinese and Japanese traditional medicine. It is attributed to **Huang Ti**, the legendary Yellow Emperor and mythical "father of Chinese medicine." The *Nei Ching* is written as a dialogue between the Yellow Emperor and his minister Ch'I Pai. The *Nei Ching* was put into writing in the 3rd century BCE, and the present form dates from the 8th century CE. In China, this is

FIGURE 7
China 1983, Sc#1847–1848. Tomb of the Yellow Emperor.

regarded as the most influential medical work in existence. The symptoms of diabetes, excessive thirst and frequent urination, are mentioned.[17]

Ancient Chinese medicine focused on the prevention of illness. Huang Ti observed, "The superior physician helps before the early budding of disease." Figure 7 shows one of a set of stamps depicting Huang Ti's tomb issued by China in 1983.

MIDDLE AGES

The period of western European history referred to as the Middle Ages extends from the time of early fragmentation and collapse of the Roman Empire, beginning around 350 CE, to about 1450 CE. No single event signaled the end of the period of antiquity and the beginning of the medieval period. The practice of medicine in the Middle Ages was fundamentally a restatement and acceptance of Greco-Roman teachings. Arabian physicians translated the works of Hippocrates and Galen and offered minor modifications. No significant advances were made in the knowledge of anatomy or physiology, as human dissections were restricted and met with social sanctions. Anatomy was frequently taught from the dissection of pigs, and rarely from a human body except to determine the cause of death. A desire for greater knowledge of human anatomy led to the revival of dissection of cadavers in the 14th century.

The medieval concept of disease was based on Hippocratic writings in the *Nature of Man*.[9] Physicians believed that disease was caused by changes in the composition of the four humors, blood, phlegm, yellow bile, and black bile, which represented various combinations of the four basic elements that were thought to compose the human organism, fire, air, earth, and water. Disease was believed to occur when the normal balance between the humors was disrupted. During fever, physicians were obliged to examine the urine for changes in color, sediment, and cloudiness.

Two prominent medieval physicians who contributed to the knowledge of diabetes in the 11th and 12th centuries were Avicenna and Moses Maimonides.

Arabian Medicine

Avicenna (Ibn Sina) (980–1037) was a Persian physician, philosopher, and astronomer known throughout the Middle Ages as the "prince of physicians" and equal of Galen. He was a prolific writer, and his attempt to organize all of the medical knowledge of his time resulted in one of the most famous medical textbooks ever written, the *Canon (Qanun) of Medicine* (Rules of Medicine), a five-volume encyclopedia.[18] Translated into Latin by Gerard of Cremona in the 12th century, the *Canon* served as a standard medical textbook in Europe until the 17th century. The introduction to the *Canon* reads, "Whoever has mastered the first book of the Qanun, to him nothing will be hidden of the general and fundamental principles of medicine."

Avicenna's knowledge of medicine was largely speculative and closely bound up in philosophy. He knew little of human anatomy, because Islamic physicians were forbidden by their religion to practice dissection. However, Avicenna knew of the sweet taste of diabetic urine and that diabetes could be primary or secondary to another disease. He described a wasting away of the body, infections, nonhealing wounds (ulcers), bone disease (osteomyelitis), and diabetic gangrene.[2,18]

FIGURE 8
Iran 1954, Sc#B32.
Portrait of Avicenna (Ibn-Sina).

Avicenna wrote, "In treating ulcers, the aim is to procure dessication, so the exposed surfaces will dry up ... ulcers in situations which are not fleshy, and round ulcers, cannot be made to heal quickly. ..." It appears that he could be describing diabetic foot ulcers. He went on to mention conditions that prevent the healing of an ulcer, and specifically referred to the role of nutrition and disease of the underlying bone. "The only remedy for this is to deal with the bone-disease: massage can help to get rid of the diseased bone, otherwise it must be excised; adductive plasters are often required for the treatment of ulcers to enable fragments of bones and foreign objects lodged in the flesh to be withdrawn, for otherwise they prevent healing."[18]

Avicenna's profile is shown in Figure 8 on a stamp issued by Iran in 1954. Avicenna is also featured on a 1987 stamp from Hungary. Figure 9 is a commemorative stamp issued by Austria in 1982 for the European Congress of Urology. The stamp depicts a medieval physician examining a sample of urine in a transparent flask. The illustration is taken from Avicenna's *Canon*.

Moses Maimonides (Rambam) (1138–1204) was a renowned medieval physician, rabbi, philosopher, theologian, and astronomer. He was well versed in the writings of Hippocrates, Galen, Aristotle, and Rhazes of Persia. Maimonides' major medical work, written in Arabic and based on the writings of Galen, was *The Medical Aphorisms of Moses*.[11] Most of the nearly 1,500 apho-

FIGURE 9
Austria 1982, Sc#1208. Urinalysis. Avicenna's Al-Qanan manuscript. European Congress of Urology, Vienna 1982.

FIGURE 10
Israel 1953, Sc#74.
Moses Maimonides. 7th
International Congress of
History and Science.

risms in this book are based on the writings of Galen. Maimonides' own original statements are preceded by "Moses says." Ancient and medieval physicians frequently wrote in the form of aphorisms, which are short concise statements of a principle. This custom can be traced to Hippocrates.

Maimonides discussed the symptoms of excessive thirst (polydipsia) and the passage of a large volume of urine (polyuria). He quoted Galen when he said, "The illness correctly called 'polyuria' is called 'diabetes (insipidus)' by many (physicians) and 'polydipsia' by many others. The patient with this illness suffers from intense thirst and drinks enormous quantities and rapidly urinates that which he drinks. The seat of this illness is in the kidneys and bladder. . . ."[11,19]

Although Galen wrote that diabetes was rare and that he had seen only two cases of this illness, Maimonides claimed to have seen more patients with diabetes. Moses says, "I too have not seen it in the West nor did any of my teachers under whom I studied mention that they had seen it. However, here in Egypt, in the course of approximately 10 years, I have seen more than twenty people who suffered from this illness. This brings one to the conclusion that this illness occurs mostly in warm countries. Perhaps the waters of the Nile, because of their sweetness, play a role in this (disease causation)."[11]

Maimonides concluded that diabetes is due to the prevailing heat, which spreads over the kidneys. Figure 10 shows a portrait of Moses Maimonides on a commemorative stamp issued by Israel in 1953 for the International Congress on the History of Science. Moses Maimonides is also featured on stamps issued by Grenada, Sierre Leone, and Spain.

No further progress was made in the understanding of diabetes until the 16th century, when the scholar Paracelsus challenged the medical doctrine of his time and attempted to reform medical thinking.

The
Diagnostic
Period

THE RENAISSANCE

The word *renaissance* literally means rebirth. This period of European history began in Italy in the 14th century and represents the humanistic revival of classical art, literature, and science and was also marked by political and religious transformations. The Renaissance, characterized by a burst of intellectual and creative activity, formed the bridge from the Middle Ages to modern times.

In medicine, there was an exhilarating revision of medical and scientific concepts beginning in the 16th century. Renaissance physicians and scientists questioned conventional thinking with a renewed spirit of curiosity, objectivity, and experimentation. Medical historian Osler noted that "This period accomplished three things in medicine, 1) it shattered authority, 2) it laid the foundation of an accurate knowledge of human anatomy, and 3) it demonstrated how the body's functions should be studied intelligently."[4] The medieval medical system began to give way as Paracelsus, Vesalius, and William Harvey, medical pioneers who had broad intellectual interests, challenged traditional dogma. They were truly "Renaissance men" who were not afraid to question conventional thinking. As a result, they were subjected to storms of criticism from

FIGURE 11
Hungary 1989,
Sc#3214. Paracelsus
1493–1541.

their contemporaries. Albert Einstein summed this up well when he said that great spirits have always encountered violent opposition from mediocre minds.

The Swiss physician Theophrastus Bombastus von Hohenheim referred to himself as **Paracelsus** (1493–1541), meaning the equal of Celsus, who was the first important Roman writer on medical history. Paracelsus was an acute observer, a profound thinker, and one of the most controversial figures of the Renaissance. He taught reliance on one's own observations, and openly rejected the doctrines of medicine proposed by the old authorities, Galen and Avicenna. In a symbolic gesture, he threw Avicenna's *Canon* into a public bonfire in front of the University of Basel. Osler described Paracelsus as the "Luther of medicine," the embodiment of the spirit of revolt.[4]

Regarded as the "father of pharmacology," Paracelsus emphasized the role of chemistry in medicine and taught that alchemy—medieval chemical science—should be applied to the treatment of disease. He believed that the human body was composed of three basic substances: sulfur, mercury, and salt. This led him to postulate that the chemical change in the body that caused diabetes was an accumulation of salt. When he evaporated a liter of diabetic urine, he recovered 4 ounces of what he thought was salt—although it was actually sugar. This experiment led Paracelsus to conclude that, ". . . when the salt in the urine comes to the kidneys, it irritates them . . . and makes the kidneys thirsty. Now the thirst always comes from the salt, thus this salt makes the kidneys salty . . . therefore it is not possible to drink enough, and as man always drinks, he floods the kidneys, which they do not excrete through the urine; for the expulsive force is not able to expel so much, therefore it does not all go into the urine, but goes into other members: thus the humor comes and swells the feet."[20]

Paracelsus prescribed anodynes for the treatment of diabetes, "for the dissolved salt & alum should be overcome." He believed that the vapor from anodynes would flow to the kidneys and extinguish the excessive thirst. A stamp was issued by Hungary in 1989 showing Paracelsus, a pair of scales, and glass flasks (Figure 11). West Germany issued a stamp featuring Paracelsus in 1949.

Belgian **Andreas Vesalius** (1514–1564) studied at the Universities of Louvain, Paris, and Padua, where he graduated in 1537 as a doctor of medicine. He demonstrated an early interest in the structure and function of the human body, and his studies revolutionized anatomy and formalized anatomic dissection.[4,21,22] Vesalius performed public dissections and challenged Galen's teachings, which until then were considered infallible. In 1543, at the age of 28, Vesalius completed a monumental, beautifully illustrated anatomical work, *De Humanis Corporis Fabrica Libri Septem*, seven books on the structure of the human body.[23,24] This elaborate work was based on his dissections of human cadavers and is the most famous anatomical work ever published.

FIGURE 12
Belgium 1964, Sc#606.
Vesalius 1514–1564
woodcut portrait from
the Fabrica.

Contrary to custom, Vesalius dissected bodies himself, acting as lecturer, demonstrator, and dissector. He employed medical students as assistants instead of barber-surgeons. The practice had been for barber-surgeons to dissect bodies, often with a meat cleaver, while a physician read aloud from the works of Galen. Vesalius' meticulous attention to anatomical detail brought to light numerous errors in Galen's anatomical treatises, which had been based largely on the dissection of lower animals such as apes and pigs.

Vesalius established modern observational science and research, which marked a turning point in the history of medicine. He is featured on a stamp issued by Belgium in 1964 commemorating the 400th anniversary of his death. The image is a famous woodcut portrait of Vesalius, showing a dissection of the right arm, from the *Fabrica* (Figure 12).

Vesalius is also shown on another Belgian stamp issued in 1942.

Although Vesalius identified the pancreas in the *Fabrica*, it is not the primary focus of the image and is very difficult to recognize. The pancreas was regarded as several glands, broken up by the dissection to expose the veins, arteries, and nerves. A comprehensive description of the pancreas and its secretions would not occur until the 17th century.

William Harvey (1578–1657) was an English physician who, like Vesalius, studied at the University of Padua. He returned to London to complete his studies at Cambridge and was elected a fellow of the College of Physicians in

FIGURE 13
Russia 1957, Sc#1947. William Harvey 1578–1657. Issued to commemorate the 300th anniversary of the death of the English physician, discoverer of the blood circulation.

1607. Harvey is considered the greatest physician of the 17th century.

Although Harvey's contribution is not specific to the history of diabetes, his work had a profound influence on the practice of medicine. Before the 17th century, it was thought that the circulation of blood consisted of two closed systems, 1) the natural circulation, which contained venous blood, originating in the liver, and 2) the vital circulation, which contained another blood and the spirits originating from the heart and provided heat and life to the body.[4] Harvey discovered the heart's role as a muscular pump propelling the blood in a circular course. He observed that the activity of the heart consisted of contraction of its fibers by which it expelled blood from the ventricles. He also noted that the pulsations in the arteries were related to the impulse of blood within the vessels, which corresponded to the heart's contractions.

Harvey's classic work, De Motu Cordis (1639), laid the foundation for modern physiology.[25] Figure 13 shows a stamp issued by Russia in 1957 commemorating the 300th anniversary of the death of William Harvey. Harvey can also be seen on stamps issued by Argentina and Hungary.

In 1664, **Regnier (Reinier) de Graaf** (1641–1673), a Dutch physician, provided the first modern description of the pancreas and its external secretions (pancreatic digestive juices). He surgically created a fistula (passageway) from the pancreas to the external surface in a dog and obtained its secretions. De Graaf's doctoral dissertation on the nature and use of pancreatic juice, Tractatus Anatomico Medicus de Succi Pancreatici Natura & Usu, was supported by his experiments draining the pancreatic secretions from dogs.[26] He believed— correctly—that pancreatic juice was a fundamental digestive secretion.

The accompanying illustration of the pancreas appears in de Graaf's monograph and is reproduced courtesy of the Malloch Rare Book Room of the New York Academy of Medicine (Figure 14).

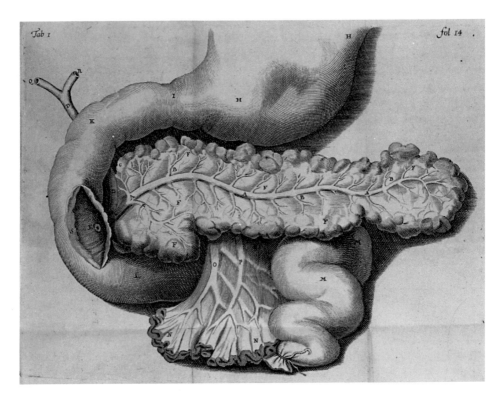

FIGURE 14
Engraved plate of the pancreas from Renier de Graaf's *Tractatus Anatomico Medicus de Succi Pancreatici Natura et Usa*, Leyden, 1671. Courtesy of the Malloch Rare Book Room of the New York Academy of Medicine. Key: H, stomach; I, pylorus; K&L, duodenum; E, ampulla; A, pancreatic duct; D, hepatic duct; O&P, superior mesenteric artery and vein.

Thomas Willis (1621–1675) was an English physician, anatomist, and Sedleian professor of natural philosophy at the University of Oxford. He provided the first modern description of cerebral neuroanatomy, the arteries at the base of the brain (circle of Willis), the cranial nerves, the spinal cord, and the peripheral and autonomic nervous systems. Willis developed the concept of neurology and coined the term *neurology* in his major work *Cerebri Anatome* (1664). [27]

One of the foremost physicians of the 17th century, Willis' knowledge and interest was not limited to neurology. In *Pharmaceutice Rationalis* (1674–1675), he wrote "Of The Too Much Evacuation By Urine, And Its Remedy; And Especially of The Diabetes or Pissing Evil, Whose Theory And Method of Curing Is Inquired Into."[28] Willis referred to diabetes as the "pissing evil" and noted that in patients with diabetes, "the urine is wonderfully sweet, as if it were imbued with honey or sugar."

He claimed that diabetes was primarily a disease of the blood and not the kidneys. Willis believed that the sweetness appeared first in the blood and was later found in the urine. He described the symptoms of polyuria and excessive thirst. "Those laboring with this Disease, piss a great deal more than they drink. Moreover they have continual thirst and gentle Fever."

FIGURE 15
Portrait of Thomas Willis at age 45. Signed engraving by R.W. Sculp, courtesy of the National Library of Medicine.

Willis observed that diabetes was no longer a rare ailment, given to the immoderate drinking of wine. "The Diabetes was a Disease so rare among the Ancients, that many famous physicians made no mention of it, and Galen knew only two sick of it; But in our age given to good fellowship and gusling down chiefly of unallayed wine; we meet with examples and instances enough, I may say daily, of this Disease."[28] In addition, Willis cited several other presumed causes of diabetes, including an ill manner of living, sadness, long grief, convulsive affections, and depression.

Willis provided what may be one of the earliest descriptions of diabetic peripheral neuropathy characterized by lancinating (sharp and shooting) pains. "I have observed in many people who have been subject to this disease . . . they felt flying, running pains through their whole Bodies, and corrugations sometimes with dizziness or stinging . . ."[27] Figure 15 is a portrait of Thomas Willis at age 45.

This is a signed engraving by R.W. Sculp, courtesy of the National Library of Medicine. No postage stamps are currently available to commemorate Willis' vast contributions to medicine.

Matthew Dobson (1735–1784) was born in Yorkshire, England, and graduated from the University of Edinburgh in 1756. Dobson was the first to demonstrate the presence of sugar in the urine and blood of patients with diabetes. He reported on nine patients who were afflicted with diabetes in which "the urine has always been sweet in a greater or less degree." Dobson detailed his findings in the paper "Experiments And Observations On The Urine In A Diabetes," which was presented to the Medical Society of London in 1776 and published that year. [29]

Dobson provided experimental evidence that people with diabetes eliminate sugar in their urine. He gently heated two quarts of urine to dryness. The remaining residue was a white cake, which Dobson wrote, "was granulated, and broke easily between the fingers; it smelled sweet like brown sugar, neither could it be distinguished from sugar, except that the sweetness left a slight sense of coolness on the palate." [29]

In another experiment, Dobson took eight ounces of blood from the arm of his patient with diabetes, and noted that, "the serum was sweetish, but I thought not as sweet as the urine. It appears that the saccharine matter (found in the urine) was not formed in the secretory organ (the kidneys), but previously existed in the serum of the blood." [29]

Dobson proposed an explanation for the emaciating effects of diabetes, which he related to such a large proportion of "alimentary matter" being excreted by the kidneys before it could be absorbed and applied to nutrition.

Thomas Willis' observations of diabetes and Matthew Dobson's experiments conclusively established the diagnosis of diabetes in the presence of sugar in the urine and blood. The term *mellitus* was soon to be adopted in the description of diabetes.

It was **William Cullen** (1710–1790), one of Britain's foremost clinicians, consultants, and educators, who was primarily responsible for introduction of the term *diabetes mellitus*.[30,31] In 1769, Cullen published an elaborate classification of human diseases titled *Synopsis Nosologiae Methodicae*.[32] In this classification, we see for the first time a distinction between diabetes (mellitus), with urine of "the smell, colour and flavour of honey," and diabetes (insipidus) with limpid but not sweet urine. It was Cullen who added the descriptive adjective *mellitus*, from the Latin word for honey, to the Greek word *diabetes*.

Matthew Dobson consulted William Cullen for an opinion of his experiments. Cullen wrote back, congratulating him on his experimental findings. "I think myself much obliged to you for the communication of your experiments and you do me a great deal of honour in asking my opinion of them. A little indisposition has given me some leisure to consider them and I give you my judgement with all the candour and freedom which friendship ought to beget. I must say in the first place that I think you have made a discovery.

FIGURE 16

Portion of a letter from William Cullen to Matthew Dobson re diabetes, circa 1775. MS Cullen 137. Courtesy of Glasgow University Library, Department of Special Collections.

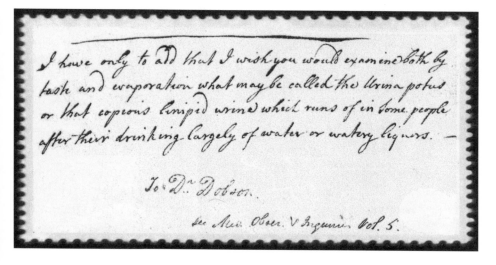

Many have taken notice of the sweet taste of the urine in the Diabetes and tho there are cases as I know certainly in which it does not occur, it was very wrong in any body to deny it altogether . . ."[33]

The letter goes on to discuss Dobson's experiments and the sweet taste of urine in diabetes. Cullen wrote, "You have done something in putting it beyond all doubt by your experiments." He concluded with a request alluding to people with diabetes insipidus. "I have only to add that I wish you would examine both by taste and evaporation what may be called urina potus or that copius limpid urine which runs of in some people after their drinking largely of water or watery liquors." Figure 16 is a portion of this letter, courtesy of the University of Glasgow, Scotland.

John Rollo (d. 1809) was an English physician and Surgeon-General to the Royal Artillery who conceived the first scientific approach to medical nutrition therapy for the treatment of diabetes. Based on his experiments, Rollo proposed a diet low in carbohydrate and high in fat and protein and shifted prevailing thinking on the cause of diabetes from the kidneys to the stomach.

FIGURE 17
Title page from John Rollo's *Cases Of The Diabetes Mellitus*, second edition, 1798. Courtesy of the National Library of Medicine.

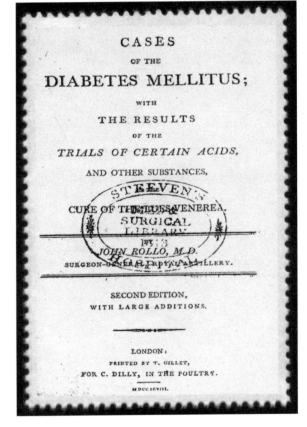

In 1798, he published *Cases Of The Diabetes Mellitus; with The Results Of The Trials of Certain Acids, And Other Substances In The Cure of the Lues Venerea* (Figure 17), in which he described the treatment of an artillery soldier, Captain Meredith, who was an obese man with adult-onset diabetes.[34,35] The patient had complaints of great thirst, keenness of appetite, and excessive urination. On examination of the urine, "it was found to be sweet." Rollo carefully recorded the quantity and types of foods eaten by Meredith and collected his excreted urine. In the manner of Thomas Dobson, the urine was evaporated to dryness, and the residue, "saccharine matter," was weighed.

Rollo's important finding was that the amount of saccharine substance urinated varied from day to day, depending on the types of foods that were eaten. "Vegetable" matter—breads, grains, and fruits—increased the amount of sugar in the urine. "Animal" matter—meat and fat—decreased the amount of sugar. This led Rollo to conclude that the immediate cause of diabetes mellitus was a condition of the stomach and to prescribe a diet of animal food to prevent the stomach's production of sugar. His prescription follows.

Breakfast	1½ pints of milk and ½ pint of lime-water, mixed together, and bread and butter
Noon	Plain blood-puddings, made of blood and suet only
Dinner	Game, or old meats, which have been long kept, and as far as the stomach may bear, fat and rancid old meats, as pork; to eat in moderation
Supper	The same as breakfast

In addition, the patient was allowed to drink only "sulfurated alkaline water" during the day and "antimonial wine" and tincture of opium at bedtime. Occasional bloodletting was also prescribed. Can you imagine trying to follow this diet? It is truly remarkable that Captain Meredith survived this treatment, became free from disease, and returned to active service in the Royal Artillery.

Later in the 19th century, during the Franco-Prussian war, the French physician **Appolinaire Bouchardat** (1806–1886) observed that, with shortages of food and rationing during the German siege on Paris, his patients with diabetes showed improvement, with a disappearance of sugar in the urine and symptoms of diabetes.[2] Bouchardat recommended fasting days and exercise for the treatment of diabetes. He advised the use of fresh vegetables, alcohol, gluten bread, and fats to substitute for carbohydrates

Severe dietary restriction, "starvation treatment," would become the only hope for management of type 1 (juvenile) diabetes. This approach to treatment would be introduced in the early 1900s by Frederick M. Allen and promoted by Elliott P. Joslin. Prior to the discovery of insulin, this extreme restriction of calories was the only approach to treatment and prevention of diabetic coma.[36]

The
Experimental
Period

T he Experimental Period in the history of diabetes
began in the first half of the 19th century with the
experiments of Claude Bernard and continues today.
Bernard discovered that the liver releases a substance
that affects blood sugar levels, and his experiments paved the
way for study of the internal secretions of other organs. His
work is considered the starting point of modern research into
the etiology and nature of diabetes.[37] At the close of the 19th
century, Oscar Minkowski demonstrated conclusively that
removal of the pancreas from dogs resulted in the production of
fatal diabetes. This was the turning point in determining the
endocrine function of the pancreas, i.e., its release of secretions
into the blood rather than through ducts to other organs.

The 20th century would be highlighted by even more exciting physiologic, therapeutic, biochemical, and pharmacologic
discoveries by Banting and Best, Abel, Sanger, the Coris,
Loubatière, Yalow and Berson, and many others. The Experimental Period is ongoing and overlaps the Therapeutic Era.

Claude Bernard (1813–1878) was a French physician and
physiologist who played a key role in the history of experimental medicine and diabetes and is considered the "father of
experimental physiology." Claude Bernard first employed the
term *internal secretion* in a lecture given in 1855 at the Collège

FIGURE 18
Transkei 1990, Sc#236.
Claude Bernard
1813–1878, The liver
produces glucose. The
conquest of diabetes
B2.4.

de France.[37] He indicated that the liver had two secretions, an external secretion of bile and an internal secretion of sugar that passed directly into the blood.

Two years later, Bernard discovered the glycogenic function of the liver. He isolated a starch-like substance, that he called *glycogen*, which was the precursor of glucose, "the internal secretion."[38] This observation established the liver's role as a vital organ in diabetes. Bernard also observed that puncture of the floor of the fourth ventricle of the brain, in experimental animals, temporarily increased the sugar content of the blood and urine.[38] For the first time, sugar in the urine was experimentally produced.

Bernard devised an experiment to determine the role of the pancreas in producing sugar in the urine (glycosuria). He tied off the pancreatic ducts of dogs or blocked the ducts with injections of melted fats that solidified at body temperature. Although these interventions caused the pancreas to degenerate and prevented normal digestion of food, Bernard was unable to experimentally produce sugar in the dogs' urine. Unfortunately, the idea of a double function of the pancreas—secretions through ducts and secretions directly into the blood—did not occur to Claude Bernard, and he discounted the pancreas' role as the cause of diabetes.

Claude Bernard is featured on a commemorative stamp issued in 1990 by Transkei showing the face of Bernard, a molecule of glucose superimposed on the liver, and the words "Claude Bernard 1813–1878, the liver produces glucose" (Figure 18). Bernard is also featured on stamps issued by Argentina and France.

Paul Langerhans (1847–1888) attended medical school at the University of Berlin, where he was a student of the famous pathologist Rudolf Virchow. His most famous histological finding, the pancreatic islets, was presented in his doctoral dissertation *Contributions to the Microscopic Anatomy of the Pancreas*, which he defended in 1869.[39]

Langerhans recognized that there was very little known about the structure of the pancreas compared to the extensive physiological information described by Bernard. Using a primitive light microscope, Langerhans set out to describe the appearance of the rabbit's pancreas. He injected the pancreatic ducts of rabbits with Berlin-blue dye, described the pancreatic duct system, and traced the ducts to the acinar glandular cells, which secrete digestive enzymes. Langerhans described a second set of mysterious cells scattered like "islands" that did not communicate directly with the excretory ducts. Langerhan's description is as follows, ". . . small cells of almost perfect homogenous content and of polygonal form, with round nuclei without nucleoli, mostly lying together in pairs or small groups."[39] He acknowledged that he did not know the function of these ductless cells. Twenty-four years later, in 1893, the French histologist Laguesse named these cells "islets of Langerhans."[37,39]

Figure 19 shows a primitive light microscope similar to that used by

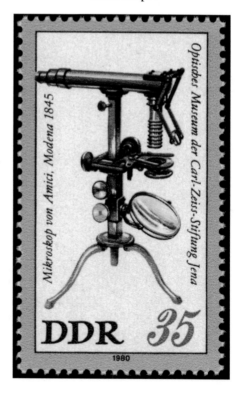

FIGURE 19
German Democratic Republic 1980, Sc#2126. Mikroskop von Amici, Moderna 1845. Monocular light microscope.

Paul Langerhans in his work. The German Democratic Republic issued the stamp, Mikroskop von Amici Moderna 1845, in 1980.

In 1889, in the laboratory of the Medical Clinic of Strassburg, **Joseph von Mering** (1849–1908) and **Oscar Minkowski** (1858–1931) made a serendipitous discovery that would prove to be one of the greatest contributions to our understanding of diabetes. Von Mering and Minkowski were curious to learn whether a dog could survive following removal of the pancreas (pancreatectomy), and if so what the effects would be on the digestion of fats and proteins. Claude Bernard had already shown that removal of the pancreas would shortly prove fatal. Minkowski, a surgeon, assisted by von Mering, removed the pancreas from a laboratory dog. Within 24 hours, the dog developed symptoms of severe diabetes: excessive hunger, abnormally increased thirst, marked polyuria, emaciation, and loss of strength, "a genuine lasting diabetes mellitus."[40]

After a series of pancreatectomies, the scientists were able to describe what happens in untreated diabetes. The sugar found in the urine of the dogs was dextrose (fermentable dextrorotary glucose); the dogs, like a person with diabetes, showed diminished ability to heal and decreased resistance to infection. In sacrificed animals, the livers of the dogs contained extremely little glycogen. Like people deprived of insulin, the dogs developed diabetic coma and died. If the pancreas was only partially removed, diabetes did not develop.

FIGURE 20
Transkei 1990, Sc#237. Oscar Minkowski 1858–1931, pancreas malfunctioning causes diabetes. The conquest of diabetes B3.4.

Figure 20 shows a commemorative stamp issued by Transkei in 1990 featuring Oscar Minkowski, and the pancreas, duodenum, and spleen.

On the heels of von Mering's and Minkowski's work, many investigators attempted to prepare extracts of the "internal secretion" of the pancreas, which they hoped would alleviate the symptoms of diabetes when administered to animals. Among these researchers were Georg Ludwig Zuelzer (1908) in Germany, E. L. Scott (1912) in the United States, and Nicholas Paulescu (1921) in Romania.[35–37,41] In 1908, Zuelzer published the results of his attempts to prepare the first pancreatic extract to suppress the appearance of glucose in the urine. Unfortunately, Zuelzer's extract had toxic side effects. While a graduate student at the University of Chicago, Scott administered pancreatic extracts to four dogs, which responded with lower levels of sugar in their urine. Scott's attempts to tie off the pancreatic ducts of dogs were unsuccessful. Paulescu came closest to discovering insulin, and his story, the less well known insulin story, will follow later.

In 1901, **Eugene Lindsay Opie** (1873–1971), a pathologist at Johns Hopkins University, described degeneration of the islets of Langerhans in people with diabetes mellitus. Opie felt there was a causal relationship between diabetes and the changes he observed in the pancreatic islets.[42] His findings established the association between failure of the islet cells and diabetes mellitus.[37]

In 1907, U.S. physician **Stanley Rossiter Benedict** (1884–1936) introduced the Benedict's solution test for urine glucose. This advance enabled physicians and people with diabetes to roughly estimate the amount of glucose in the urine.[43] When heated in the presence of a sugar such as glucose, Benedict's solution changes from its normal blue color to red, yellow, or green depending on the concentration of the glucose. It quickly became common for people with diabetes to test their urine at home using Benedict's solution: eight to ten drops of urine were added to five milliliters of this agent, heated, and

FIGURE 21
Belgium 1971, Sc#811. 50th anniversary of the discovery of insulin. Benedict's test for urine glucose and a molecule of proinsulin. White circles represent C-peptide. Black circles represent a molecule of insulin, two chains of amino acids connected by two disulfide bonds.

allowed to cool slowly. The resulting color was compared to a color chart.

Belgium issued this colorful stamp in 1971 to commemorate the 50th anniversary of the discovery of insulin (Figure 21). The test tubes represent Benedict's test for the measurement of urine glucose. Also depicted on this stamp is a molecule of proinsulin. (Please look for a discussion of proinsulin, C-peptide, and the insulin molecule in The Therapeutic Era.)

J. de Mayer was the first to propose the name *insuline* for the hypothetical internal secretion of the pancreas in 1909, followed independently by **Sir Edward Albert Sharpy-Schafer** in 1916.[37] Both men based the name on the Latin word for island, *insula*. Schafer proposed that the substance necessary for carbohydrate metabolism was produced in the islets of Langerhans.

THE AGE OF INSULIN

The discovery of insulin at the University of Toronto in 1921–1922 was one of the greatest events in the history of medicine. Insulin therapy commuted the death sentence associated with the diagnosis of type 1 diabetes. Michael Bliss brilliantly described the events leading up to this scientific discovery in his book *The Discovery of Insulin*, to which I refer you for the full story.[36]

Frederick Grant Banting (1891–1941) was a Canadian who attended medical school at the University of Toronto. Following military service in World War I, he completed his surgical training and opened his office in London, Ontario.[12] Banting had been only an average student and was a very

FIGURE 22
Canada 1999, Sc#1822a. Frederick G. Banting, Charles H. Best, page from Banting's research notebook.

unlikely scientist. He trained as an orthopedic surgeon and had no formal instruction in research. To supplement his income, Banting had a part-time teaching appointment, as a demonstrator in surgery and anatomy, at the Western University in London, Ontario. It was in this capacity that he developed an interest in carbohydrate metabolism.

Bliss wrote that Banting's research interests were stimulated by an article published in November 1920 in which author Moses Barron described a patient with a rare case of a pancreatic stone that blocked the main pancreatic duct.[44] The blockage resulted in degeneration of the acinar glandular cells that secreted into the duct but not the islet cells. It occurred to Banting that if he were to tie off the pancreatic duct, he might be able to obtain the internal secretion of the pancreas, free from the external secretion. Banting recorded the following words in his research notebook as he planned his experimental approach to obtaining the internal secretion of the pancreas, and a cure for diabetes:

"Diabetus
Ligate pancreatic ducts of dog. Keep dogs alive till acini degenerate leaving islets. Try to isolate the internal secretion of these to relieve glycosurea."[36]

These words can be seen on a commemorative stamp issued by Canada in 1999. In addition, the stamp shows the images of Frederick G. Banting, Charles Best, a dog with pancreas removed, and an insulin syringe (Figure 22). The spelling errors (Diabetus and glycosurea) are Banting's. It goes to show that brilliance and success are not necessarily tied to spelling proficiency.

Despite initial rebuffs by **John James Rickard Macleod** (1876–1935), professor of physiology at the University of Toronto, the persistent Fred Banting was finally allowed to begin his research, without pay, in Macleod's laboratory in May 1921. Macleod, a Scotsman, was a highly respected physiologist and expert in the area of carbohydrate metabolism. He doubted that Banting would be able to isolate the internal secretion of the pancreas because of the destructive effects of the pancreatic juice. Nevertheless, Banting was assigned laboratory space, research animals, and a 22-year-old research assistant named **Charles Herbert Best** (1899–1978). Best had just graduated from the University of Toronto with a Bachelor of Arts degree, having taken an honors course in physiology and biochemistry. His goal was to work for Professor Macleod while pursuing a Master's degree in physiology.

Macleod recruited biochemist **James Bertram Collip** (1892–1965) to help Banting and Best isolate the internal secretion using modern biochemistry techniques. Together, they set out to obtain a pancreatic extract and to succeed where many others had failed. By November 1921, they had developed a procedure to prevent the destructive effect of pancreatic enzymes on "the active principle of the extract." In their first paper, Banting and Best reported that they had administered more than 75 doses of their pancreatic extract "Isletin" to 10 dogs made diabetic by surgery and demonstrated a dramatic reduction in urinary and blood sugar.[45] They also observed a noticeable improvement in the overall condition of the dogs after administration of Isletin.

In March 1922, Banting and Best published a preliminary report of the administration of Isletin in seven cases of human diabetes. They presented the case report of a 14-year-old boy on death's doorstep. The youngster, identified as L.T., was admitted to Toronto

FIGURE 23
Canada 1971, Sc#533. 50th anniversary of the discovery of insulin. Laboratory equipment from Banting and Best's laboratory at the University of Toronto.

General Hospital poorly nourished, weighing 65 pounds, and with the smell of acetone (associated with ketoacidosis) on his breath. L.T. would later be known worldwide as Leonard Thompson, the first person to be treated with insulin. Thompson would live for another 13 years, before succumbing to pneumonia and severe acidosis.[46]

In their report, Banting and Best concluded that blood glucose could be markedly reduced, even to normal values; glucose in the urine could be abolished; acetone bodies could be made to disappear from the urine; and a definite improvement was observed in the overall condition of their patients. Figure 23 shows laboratory equipment (Duboscq colorimeter, beaker, test tubes, vial of insulin, and syringe) from Frederick Banting's laboratory. This Canadian stamp was issued in 1971 to commemorate the 50th anniversary of the discovery of insulin. The Duboscq colorimeter was an important laboratory instrument that enabled Banting and Best to accurately measure blood glucose using a small sample of blood.

Banting's portrait is also shown on a stamp issued by Transkei in 1990 (Figure 24). This is the fourth stamp in a set of four stamps commemorating the conquest of diabetes. Also shown on the stamp are a dog with pancreas removed, a syringe, vial of pancreatic extract, and a line graph showing reduction in urine or blood glucose following administration of the extract.

Banting and Best succeeded in their experiments, where Zuelzer,

FIGURE 24
Transkei 1990, Sc#238. Frederick Banting 1891–1941, discoverer of insulin. The conquest of diabetes B4.4.

Scott, and Paulescu had failed, due to a combination of circumstances: good science, good luck, great enthusiasm, motivation, and determination. They were fortunate to have available to them the resources of the University of Toronto, the scientific knowledge and prestige of Macleod, and the biochemistry skills of Collip. In addition, they had modern surgical techniques and laboratory procedures for the accurate measurement of glucose, nitrogen, and ketone bodies in small samples of blood and urine.[47]

The figures that history has most closely associated with the discovery of insulin are Frederick G. Banting and Charles H. Best. Yet, the 1923 Nobel Prize in Medicine or Physiology was not awarded to Banting and Best, but to Banting and Macleod.[48] This did not sit well with Banting, who expressed strong resentment toward Macleod. Bliss noted that Banting was so furious that he initially refused to accept the prize rather than share the honor with Macleod. In an attempt to remedy this injustice, Banting publicly acknowledged Best's role in the discovery of insulin and shared the monetary prize with him. Macleod agreed to do the same with Collip. Banting was the first Canadian to win a Nobel Prize.

Fifty years after the discovery of insulin, Uruguay and Kuwait issued commemorative World Health Day stamps, attributing the discovery of insulin to Banting and Best. Uruguay's stamp shows a flask with the words "Descubierta Por Banting Y Best" and the World Health Organization emblem (Figure 25). Kuwait's stamp

FIGURE 25
Uruguay 1972, Sc#C385. 50th anniversary of the discovery of insulin by Banting and Best. WHO emblem, International Year of Health.

FIGURE 26
Kuwait 1971,
Sc#523–524. 50th
anniversary of the discovery of the discovery of insulin, Charles H.
Best born 1899, and Sir
F.G. Banting 1891–1941.
World Health Day
Kuwait. WHO emblem.

features the likeness of Banting and Best with an insulin syringe, vial of insulin, and the World Health Organization emblem (Figure 26).

On February 20, 1941, Frederick Banting died in a plane crash in Newfoundland. In 1991, Canada issued a stamp commemorating the life of Sir Frederick G. Banting, 1891–1941, Physician and Researcher (Figure 27).

FIGURE 27
Canada 1991, Sc#1304.
Sir Frederick G. Banting, 1891–1941. Physician and researcher.

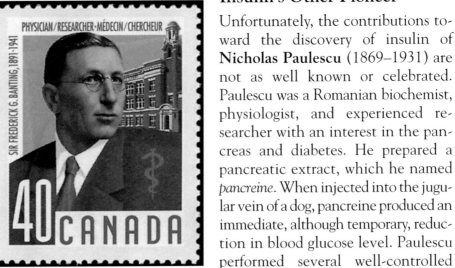

Insulin's Other Pioneer

Unfortunately, the contributions toward the discovery of insulin of **Nicholas Paulescu** (1869–1931) are not as well known or celebrated. Paulescu was a Romanian biochemist, physiologist, and experienced researcher with an interest in the pancreas and diabetes. He prepared a pancreatic extract, which he named *pancreine*. When injected into the jugular vein of a dog, pancreine produced an immediate, although temporary, reduction in blood glucose level. Paulescu performed several well-controlled experiments showing that injection of this extract reduced not only blood glucose levels, but also urine levels of glucose and ketones. He published his findings in the August 1921 issue of the *Archives Internationales de Physiologie*. Despite the fact that Paulescu published his findings before the Toronto scientists, he failed to gain recognition for his contribution to the discovery of insulin, a point of contention for the Romanians ever since.[49-51] Romania issued a stamp honoring Paulescu in 1994 (Figure 28).

FIGURE 28
Romania 1994, Sc#3966. Nicholas Paulescu 1869–1931. The other side of the insulin story.

The Therapeutic Era

The Therapeutic Era in the history of diabetes dawned in the 1920s with the discovery, isolation, purification, and therapeutic use of insulin. This was followed by the introduction of long-acting protamine zinc insulin in 1936, and the serendipitous discovery of the sulfonylureas during World War II. In 1957, G. Unger introduced the oral agent phenethylbiguanide (phenformin), which treats diabetes by decreasing the liver's release of glucose; however, this drug had the potentially

FIGURE 29
Postal cancellation, 1971. British Diabetic Association. 50th year of insulin in diabetic research. DEFEAT DIABETES IN 1971.

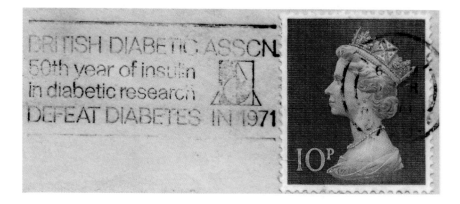

fatal toxic effect of lactic acidosis. The cry to "Defeat Diabetes" soon resonated around the world (Figure 29). Human insulin (Humulin and Novolin) became available in the early 1980s and was the first major commercial product developed by recombinant DNA technology. Metformin, a safer biguanide, was introduced in the United States in 1995. This was followed in the late 1990s by the release of several novel oral agents (insulin secretagogues and sensitizers, and alpha-glucosidase inhibitors) for the treatment of type 2 diabetes.

MAKING INSULIN AVAILABLE

In 1922, the University of Toronto issued to the Eli Lilly Company a one-year exclusive license to make insulin. Because of this early start in the insulin business, Lilly played a very important role in the development of methods for insulin production in America.[36] Lilly's insulin preparations were made from pork and called *Iletin*. Slaughterhouse pancreases of cows and pigs were the only source of insulin for many years. The pig therefore has played an important role in the history of diabetes, as

FIGURE 30
Finland 1998,
Sc#B260–262. Finland
Red Cross.

a source of insulin and life for people with diabetes. Finland issued a set of three stamps featuring pigs, for the Red Cross, in 1998 (Figure 30).

August Steenberg Krogh (1874–1949) was a distinguished professor of physiology at the University of Copenhagen who was awarded the Nobel Prize in Medicine or Physiology in 1920 "for his discovery of the capillary motor regulating mechanism."[52] Krogh observed that active muscles have more open capillaries than do less active ones. He also noted that capillaries contract or dilate in proportion to a tissue's oxygen needs.

August Krogh was invited to speak at Yale University in 1922. Krogh traveled to the United States with his wife Marie, who was a physician and reportedly had diabetes. They decided to take a side trip to the University of Toronto to visit Frederick Banting and J.J.R. Macleod. The Kroghs were familiar with Banting's research and his discovery of insulin and hoped to secure permission to produce insulin in Scandinavia. Permission was granted, and they returned home to start work. With financial backing from **August Kongsted**, Krogh and **Hans Christian Hagedorn** began insulin production, and in March 1923 treated their first patients with Insulin Leo. Shortly thereafter, they established the Nordisk Insulin Laboratory. In 1924, Nordisk became an independent nonprofit institution. In 1925, Novo Terapeutisk Laboratory was formed, and Denmark had two firms that were to become leading manufacturers of insulin. In January 1989, Nordisk and Novo joined under the name Novo Nordisk A/S.[53]

FIGURE 31
Sweden 1980, Sc#1342.
Nobel Prize 1920,
August Steenberg Krogh.

Sweden issued a stamp in 1980 picturing Krogh at work in his laboratory, commemorating his 1920 Nobel Prize (Figure 31).

UNDERSTANDING INSULIN'S STRUCTURE

John Jacob Abel (1857–1938), a physician, biochemist, and professor of pharmacology at Johns Hopkins University, is considered the "founding father of pharmacology" in the United States. Abel discovered the first hormone, adrenaline (epinephrine), in 1898. He purified insulin and isolated its crystalline structure in 1926. The beautiful rhombohedral crystals of insulin fascinated Abel. His studies of insulin helped to develop modern concepts of protein chemistry.[54] Insulin crystals are featured on stamps issued by Denmark and by Japan. Denmark's stamp was issued in 1990 to commemorate the 50th anniversary of the Danish Diabetes Association 1940–1990 (Figure 32).

Japan's stamp was issued in 1994 to commemorate the 15th International Diabetes Federation Congress, held in Kobe that year (Figure 33).

Frederick Sanger (1918–), a British biochemist at Cambridge University, was the first to discover the complete amino acid sequence of a protein—insulin. Sanger was awarded the 1958 Nobel Prize in Chemistry "for his work on the structure of proteins, especially that of insulin." With his new methods for amino acid sequencing, Sanger determined that the insulin molecule was composed of two different chains

FIGURE 32
Denmark 1990, Sc#B75.
Insulin Crystals. 50th
anniversary Danish
Diabetes Association.

of amino acids held together by two bridges of sulfur atoms. He gave the exact sequence of the 31 amino acids in one chain and the 20 in the other.[55]

Insulin is produced by pancreatic beta cells within the islets as a single-chain polypeptide prohormone called proinsulin. To become the active hormone, this single chain of amino acids is chemically broken into two portions: the two-chain hormone insulin, and a 31–amino acid fragment called *connecting peptide*, or C-peptide. Donald Steiner, at the University of Chicago, discovered proinsulin with its C-peptide in 1967. A molecule of proinsulin is represented on a 1971 postage stamp from Belgium (Figure 21, p. 36). Insulin's two chains of amino acids (A and B chains) are shown by the black circles. C-peptide is represented by the white circles. Two disulfide bonds link the two chains. Because C-peptide is split from the proinsulin molecule to produce insulin, C-peptide levels are a reliable indicator of whether a person's pancreas is producing insulin.

Sanger later became interested in nucleic acids, the building blocks of DNA, and applied some of the same chemistry concepts to study DNA. In 1977, his work resulted in the first complete determination of the sequence of components of a DNA molecule, from a bacterial virus called phi-X174. For this, he won the Nobel Prize in Chemistry for the second time, in 1980.[56] Sanger shared this honor with **Walter Gilbert** (1932–) "for their contributions concerning the determination of base

FIGURE 33
Japan 1994, Sc#2433.
Insulin crystals.
International Diabetes
Federation Congress,
15th Congress, Kobe.

sequences in nucleic acids," and with **Paul Berg** (1926–) "for his fundamental studies of the biochemistry of nucleic acids, with particular regard to recombinant-DNA." Sanger's seminal discovery of how to sequence DNA marked the beginning of the modern history of genetics and has given us the ability to decode the human genome. In fact, his sequencing method is being used today to determine the nucleic acid sequence of human DNA. The implication of Sanger's discovery rests in our ability to determine the inherited components of diseases, diabetes in particular, and to develop more effective treatment strategies.

UNDERSTANDING GLUCOSE

Carl Ferdinand Cori (1896–1984) and **Gerty Theresa Radnitz Cori** (1896–1957) attended medical school at the German University of Prague and immigrated to the United States in 1922. They were partners in life as well as in the biochemistry laboratory. Their research on carbohydrate metabolism at Washington University in St. Louis has had a profound influence on the treatment of diabetes. The Coris synthesized glycogen in the laboratory and provided an understanding of how

FIGURE 34
Gabon 1995, Sc#803a
Sheetlet III. Carl and
Gerty Cori. Nobel Prize
in Medicine or
Physiology 1947.

glucose is converted into glycogen and stored in muscle and liver for future use. This process is known as the Cori Cycle.

Carl and Gerty Cori received the 1947 Nobel Prize in Medicine or Physiology "for their discovery of the course of the catalytic conversion of glycogen." [57] Gerty Cori became the first American woman and the third woman worldwide to receive a Nobel Prize in the sciences. Bernardo A. Houssay shared the Nobel Prize "for his discovery of the part played by the hormone of the anterior pituitary lobe in the metabolism of sugar." The Republic of Gabon issued a sheetlet of stamps in 1995 commemorating the 100th Anniversary of the Nobel Prize. Carl and Gerty Cori are individually represented on two stamps, with the profile of Alfred Nobel in the background (Figure 34).

NEW WAYS TO LOWER GLUCOSE LEVELS

Oral blood glucose–lowering agents, effective for the treatment of type 2 diabetes, were discovered by chance in the early 1940s. **Auguste Loubatières** (1912–1977) was professor of medicine at the University of Montpellier during the German occupation. While studying the effects of long-acting insulin (IPZ) on depancreatized dogs, he observed prolonged low blood glucose levels (hypoglycemia), followed by convulsions, coma, and death. At the same time, his colleague **Marcel Janbon** was studying how to use the bacteria-inhibiting sulfonamide drug 2254 RP. Sulfonamides were used during World War II for the treatment of a variety of infectious diseases, among them typhoid fever. Of the 30 patients treated by Janbon, 3 died due to prolonged hypoglycemia. Loubatières recognized the similarity between the deaths of Janbon's patients and his own laboratory animals. Between 1942 and 1946, Auguste Loubatières confirmed the glucose-lowering action of sulfonamides in a series of animal experiments. He determined that the hypoglycemic effect only occurred if the animal had an intact pancreas. Loubatières con-

cluded that sulfonamides exerted blood glucose–lowering effects by stimulating the pancreas to release insulin.

France issued a stamp in 1940 to recognize the work of the French Red Cross, Pour nos Blesses (For our Wounded) (Figure 35). The stamp depicts the conditions in the south of France during World War II, at the time of Janbon's and Loubatières' investigations.[59,60] A wounded soldier is shown being comforted by a nurse.

World War II and the rebuilding of Europe following the war interrupted further development of the sulfonylurea drugs. It wasn't until 1956 that the first sulfonylurea, tolbutamide, was approved for the treatment of type 2 diabetes. This oral drug possessed unequivocal hypoglycemic properties. In 1966, glibenclamide (glyburide), a more potent, prolonged-acting "second generation" sulfonylurea became available.

MEASURING INSULIN AND OTHER HORMONES

Rosalyn Sussman Yalow (1921–) was born in New York City, where she attended Hunter College, then graduate school at the University of Illinois, where she obtained a doctorate in nuclear physics. In 1947, she became a consultant at the Bronx Veterans Administration Hospital, where she helped to set up the VA's first Radioisotope Service. In 1950, Yalow began research collaboration with **Solomon A. Berson**. Their first studies together were in the clinical application of radioisotopes, which attach to proteins and emit radiation. Proteins "labeled" with a radioisotope can be "seen," and therefore measured. They applied their methods to small peptide hormones, of which insulin was the hormone most readily available.

In the mid 1950s, Yalow and Berson made the surprising discovery that people who had received injections of animal insulin developed antibodies to the hormone. This observation was contrary to the prevailing opinion that such a small protein as insulin could not be antigenic. Yalow and Berson developed a tool with the potential for measuring insulin circulating in the blood. In a number of articles published between 1956 and 1960, they reported on the radioimmunological assay (RIA) for quantitative analysis of extremely low concentrations of peptide hormones. This became the starting point for RIA determination of insulin. The era of RIA began in 1959 and marked an important innovation in biological and medical research. Yalow received the 1977 Nobel Prize in Medicine or Physiology for "the development of radioimmunoassays of peptide hormones."[61,62] Sadly, Sol Berson died in 1972 and was unable to receive the Nobel Prize, because it is not awarded posthumously. Yalow shared half of the Nobel Prize with Roger Guillemin and Andrew Schally for their discoveries concerning "the peptide hormone production in the brain." Rosalyn

Le250

Rosalyn Yalow - Nobel Prize for Medicine - 1977 USA

SIERRA LEONE

FIGURE 36
Sierra Leone 1995, Sc#1844c. Rosalyn Sussman Yalow. Nobel Prize for Medicine 1977 USA. Radioimmunoassay.

Yalow is portrayed on a 1994 stamp issued by Sierre Leone to commemorate her 1977 Nobel Prize (Figure 36).

MEASURING BLOOD GLUCOSE

The introduction of blood glucose meters in the early 1970s marked a revolution in diabetes care. **Anton H. Clemens** invented the first blood glucose meter, the Ames Reflectance Meter (A.R.M.).[63] Clemens was an engineer with the Ames Division of Miles Laboratories when he developed a light meter that could read reflected light from paper test strips. The test strip changed color when a drop of blood was applied to the strip: the darker the blue, the higher the glucose level of the blood. Visual matching of the test strip color to a color chart provided only a rough measurement. However, accuracy of the measurement was greatly improved by use of a reflectance meter. Clemen's original meter had an analog scale with a sweep needle and a rechargeable lead acid battery; it weighed nearly two pounds. Although initially intended for use in doctors' offices, meters were soon made available for home use.

Finally, people with diabetes could easily monitor the effects of their lifestyle on blood glucose levels and make necessary adjustments to their diet, exercise, and medication dose. Until this time, self-monitoring meant testing urine glucose. Glucose levels in the urine reflect blood glucose levels of the past several hours, and so are of little use in adjusting diet or medication or preventing low glucose due to exercise. In contrast, glucose meters provide immediate feedback. This tool helped people to achieve specific blood glucose targets and to prevent and recognize hypoglycemia and hyperglycemia.

St. Vincent issued a stamp in 1989 to raise awareness of diabetes self-monitoring of blood glucose (SMBG). This was a commemorative issue for the 25th anniversary of the Lions Club of Saint Vincent. The stamp shows a finger stick and blood glucose meter (Figure 37). Today, there are more than two dozen blood glucose meters on the market. Modern meters

FIGURE 37
St. Vincent 1989,
Sc#1306. 25th
Anniversary Lions Club
of St. Vincent 1989.
Blood glucose
monitoring. Diabetes
awareness.

weigh just a few ounces, are powered by miniature batteries, and have digital displays. Most have memory features and the ability to download blood glucose data to a computer. The first meters required a large drop of blood, but sample size has decreased to just a few microliters, and test results are given in as little as 15 to 40 seconds.

The Era of Complications

The discovery and therapeutic introduction of insulin in the 1920s was a miraculous development in the treatment of diabetes that enabled individuals affected by this disease to live an almost normal life. It soon became apparent, however, that insulin did not cure diabetes. As people began to live longer, they experienced complications that had not previously been seen. Elliot P. Joslin noted, "The era of coma as the central problem of diabetes has given way to the era of complications."[36]

People with diabetes are at increased risk for the development of serious complications, including blindness, kidney failure, heart disease, stroke, and amputations. The good news is that these complications are preventable. Scientific evidence demonstrates that much of the morbidity and mortality of diabetes can be reduced by aggressive treatment with diet, exercise, and improved blood glucose control.[64,65] Diabetes self-management education is the cornerstone of care for all people with diabetes (Figure 38). Unfortunately, there is still a significant disparity between current and desired diabetes care and practices. Public awareness of the serious nature of diabetes and its complications remains very limited, despite the fact that diabetes mellitus is one of the leading causes of death and disability in the United States.

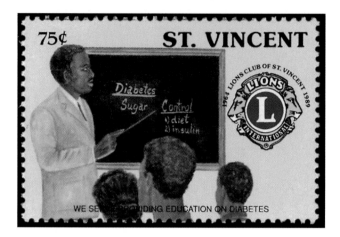

FIGURE 38
St. Vincent 1989,
Sc#1305. 25th
Anniversary Lions Club
of St. Vincent 1989.
Diabetes education.

FIGURE 39
USA 2001, Sc#3503.
Know More About
Diabetes. First U.S.
Postal Service stamp for
diabetes awareness.
Courtesy of the United
States Postal Service.
Issued March 16, 2001.

The message to "Know More About Diabetes" is seen on a stamp issued March 16, 2001, by the United States Postal Service (Figure 39, courtesy of the United States Postal Service). This first class 34-cent stamp depicts an eye, test tube, and microscope. It is the first U.S. stamp to

highlight diabetes. Brazil issued a very colorful diabetes awareness stamp in 1992, for National Diabetes Day. The stamp features a hummingbird in flight (Figure 40). Mexico issued
a diabetes awareness stamp in 2000 to commemorate the
50th anniversary of the International Diabetes Federation
Congress.

In 1993, the landmark Diabetes Control and Complications Trial (DCCT) firmly established a conclusive
relationship between chronic high blood glucose levels and
the development of complications of the eyes, nerves, and
kidneys in people with type 1 diabetes.[64] The DCCT showed
that intensive insulin therapy reduced the risk of developing retinopathy, neuropathy, and nephropathy by approximately 60% compared with conventional therapy. In 1998, the

United Kingdom Prospective Diabetes Study (UKPDS) verified similar findings in people with type 2 diabetes.[66] There was a 25% decrease in microvascular complications in subjects receiving intensive therapy versus conventional therapy.

DIABETIC EYE DISEASE

FIGURE 41
Austria 1979, Sc#1130. Diabetic eye disease—retinopathy. International Diabetes Federation Congress 1979.

Diabetes is the leading cause of new cases of blindness in adults aged 20 to 74 years old. The prevalence of retinopathy is strongly related to the duration of diabetes and uncontrolled high glucose levels. After 20 years of diabetes, nearly all

people with type 1 diabetes and nearly two-thirds of people with type 2 diabetes have some evidence of diabetic retinopathy. Diabetic retinopathy is represented on a stamp issued by Austria in 1979 for the International Diabetes Federation Congress (Figure 41). The retinal vessels are shown with areas of ischemia. Screening for diabetic retinopathy and timely treatment with laser photocoagulation surgery can prevent vision loss. Israel issued a stamp in 1988 showing the use of a laser for retinal photocoagulation surgery (Figure 42).

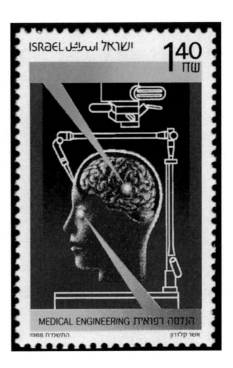

FIGURE 42
Israel 1988, Sc#981.
Medical engineering.
Laser for photo-
coagulation surgery.

DIABETIC KIDNEY DISEASE

Diabetes is the leading cause of end-stage renal disease (ESRD) in the United States and Europe. ESRD is defined as kidney failure requiring dialysis or kidney transplantation. Diabetic nephropathy accounts for more than 42% of all new cases of ESRD. The DCCT and the UKPDS have shown conclusively that intensive diabetes therapy significantly reduces the risk of developing kidney disease in people with diabetes.

Austria issued a stamp in 1990 for the European Congress of Dialysis and Transplantation (Figure 43). The stamp illustrates the anatomy of the kidney, a dialysis machine, and a transplanted kidney. The earliest evidence of kidney disease is the appearance of albumin in the urine. This finding may also serve as a marker for increased cardiovas-

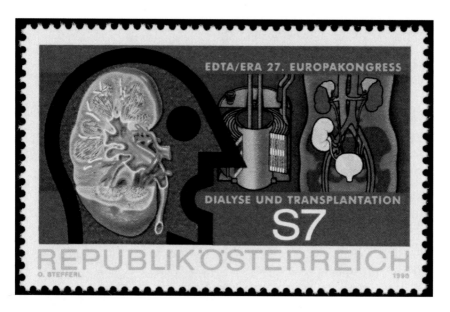

FIGURE 43
Austria 1990, Sc#1515. 27 European Congress, Dialysis and Kidney Transplantation.

cular risk. Annual screening for microalbuminuria is recommended. The rate of progression of nephropathy can be slowed by better control of blood glucose and aggressive treatment of high blood pressure (hypertension). Figure 44 shows a stamp issued by the Dominican Republic in 1974, "Lucha Contra Diabetes," Fight Against Diabetes, that portrays kidney disease.

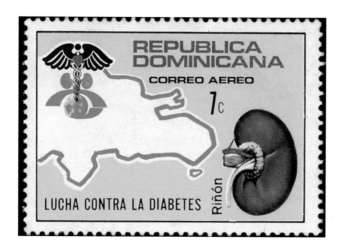

FIGURE 44
Dominican Republic 1974, Sc#C218. Fight Against Diabetes. Nephropathy.

DIABETIC CARDIOVASCULAR DISEASE

Abundant evidence shows that people with diabetes are at high risk for cardiovascular disease: coronary heart disease (CHD), stroke, peripheral arterial disease, cardiomyopathy, and microvascular disease. Heart disease is the leading cause of diabetes-related deaths and hospitalizations. Adults with diabetes have heart disease death rates about two to four times as high as

FIGURE 45
Dominican Republic
1979, Sc#811.
Dominican Institute of
Cardiology. Cardio-
vascular disease.

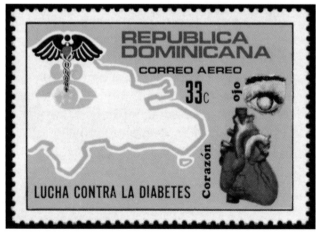

FIGURE 46
Dominican Republic
1974, Sc#C219. Fight
Against Diabetes.
Retinopathy and
cardiovascular disease.

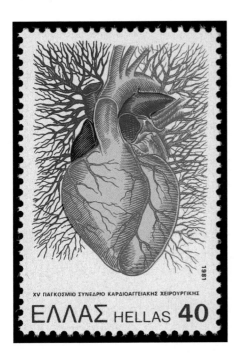

FIGURE 47
Greece 1981, Sc#1836.
15th Cardiovascular
Surgery Conference.
Heart and vessels.

those of adults without diabetes. Therefore, having diabetes is itself a risk factor for developing cardiovascular disease. The risk of stroke is two to four times higher in people with diabetes. Figure 45 shows a heart and diseased blood vessels. This stamp was issued by the Dominican Republic to commemorate the Dominican Institute of Cardiology. The Dominican Republic also issued a diabetes awareness stamp in its series "Lucha Contra Diabetes," Fight Against Diabetes, calling attention to cardiovascular disease. The eye, heart, and large blood vessels are illustrated (Figure 46). Greece issued a stamp showing the heart and great vessels to commemorate the 15th Cardiovascular Surgery Conference in 1981 (Figure 47).

DIABETIC LOWER LIMB AMPUTATIONS

In 1934, **Elliot P. Joslin** (1869–1962), physician and diabetes specialist, wrote a paper, "The Menace of Diabetic Gangrene," published in the *New England Journal of Medicine*.[66] Joslin noted that following the introduction of insulin, mortality from diabetic coma had fallen significantly from 60 percent to 5 percent. Yet, deaths from diabetic gangrene (of the foot and leg) had risen significantly. The reason, Joslin alleged, for this complication was that physicians were not aggressive enough in their treatment of diabetes. He quoted Frederick M. Allen as saying, "the surest way to produce gangrene is to keep patients alive but only half treat them." Joslin observed that gangrene increased with the age of the individual and the duration of diabetes. There was almost always a history of injury to the foot that could be elicited from the patient. Burns and ill-fitting shoes caused the most common injuries.

Joslin firmly believed that gangrene and amputations were preventable. Hopefulness in the treatment of gangrene was possible. He remarked, "It has been forced upon me that gangrene is not Heaven-sent but is earth-born." His remedy was a team approach to diabetes care, which included patient education in foot care, medical nutrition therapy, exercise, prompt treatment of foot infections, and when necessary, specialized surgical care. Joslin stressed the importance of cleanliness, daily foot inspection for early signs of trouble, and podiatric care. These tenets of care are just as applicable today.

In the 20th century, more than half of all nontraumatic lower limb amputations were performed on people with diabetes. In 1974, the Dominican Republic issued a stamp in the series "Fight Against Diabetes" to raise awareness of diabetic amputations.

FIGURE 48
Dominican Republic
1974, Sc#725–726.
Fight Against Diabetes.
Amputation.

The stamp depicts a man in a wheel chair, with an amputation of his right leg. In the upper left corner is a caduceus (rod of Hermes) with a heart and kidneys (Figure 48). In 1996, there were approximately 86,000 lower limb amputations performed on people with diabetes in the United States; 85% of these amputations are thought to have been preceded by a nonhealing foot ulcer.

The
Future

In its 1998 report, the Congressionally mandated Diabetes Research Working Group recognized the great urgency and extraordinary opportunities facing us today in diabetes research.[67] Finding a cure for diabetes and developing more effective treatments must be a national priority. An exciting area of research in the 21st century involves the genetics of diabetes. Both type 1 and type 2 diabetes and their complications have a strong genetic basis. Type 1 diabetes is an example of a T cell–mediated autoimmune disease characterized by selective destruction of a single cell type, the insulin-producing beta cells. There is a complex interaction of genetic and environmental factors. The genetic component of type 2 diabetes is thought to involve the interactions of multiple genes and environmental factors. Better understanding of the molecular basis of disease is an important purpose of human genome research. If we can find the genes that cause diabetes, we can hopefully find ways to cure the disease.

The beginning of the modern era of molecular biology began in 1953 with the discovery of the double helix structure of DNA by **James D. Watson** (1928–) and **Francis H.C. Crick** (1916–).[68] Sanger's method for the sequencing of the nucleotides in DNA in 1977 marked the beginning of the

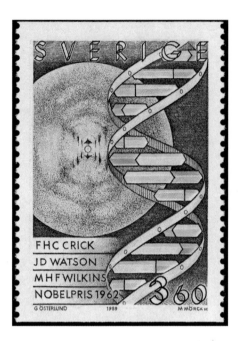

FIGURE 49
Sweden 1989, Sc#1773.
Crick, Watson, and
Wilkins, Nobel Prize
1962. DNA double helix.

modern history of DNA sequencing and our ability to decode the human genome.

The 1962 Nobel Prize in Medicine or Physiology was awarded to Crick, Watson, and **Maurice H.F. Wilkins** (1916–) "for their discoveries concerning the molecular structure of nucleic acids and its significance for information transfer in living material."[69] Sweden issued a stamp in 1989 to commemorate this accomplishment (Figure 49), showing the structure of DNA. There are two helical chains, each coiled around the same axis. Four organic bases hold the two chains together, like the rungs of a ladder. Watson and Crick found that only specific pairs of bases could bond together, to spell out the genetic code. The genetic code is spelled out by: adenine (A), thymine (T), guanine (G), and cytosine (C). A pairs with T, and G pairs with C to form the rungs of the ladder. The pairing of these bases is depicted in a commemorative stamp issued by Sweden in 1989, recognizing the 1978 Nobel Prize in Medicine or Physiology given to W. Arber, D. Nathans, and H.O. Smith "for the discovery of restriction enzymes and their application to problems of molecular genetics" (Figure 50). The United Kingdom commemorated Crick's accomplishment with a First Day Cover (FDC), "Decoding DNA," issued in 1999. The FDC shows Crick, a fetus encircled by DNA, and a millennium stamp cancelled on August 3, 1999 (Figure 51). The implication is that DNA holds the secrets of life, evolution, and hereditary diseases, such as diabetes.

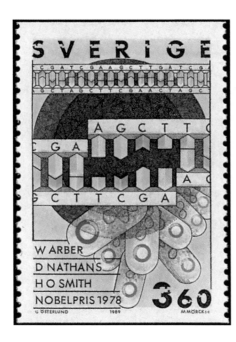

FIGURE 50
Sweden 1989, Sc#1774. Arber, Nathans, and Smith, Nobel Prize 1978. Discovery of restriction enzymes, chemical knives for cutting DNA. Stamp illustrates genetic code spelled out with specific pairs of purine and pyrimidine bases: adenine (A) with thymine (T), and guanine (G) with cytosine (C).

Francis Collins, a geneticist who is leading the National Institutes of Health and Department of Energy's Human Genome Project, noted that decoding the information embedded in the human genome will revolutionize the practice of medicine in the 21st century. [70] Begun in 1990, sequencing of the human genome was completed in 2000. Scientists discovered that there are only 30,000–40,000 genes in the human genome, not 100,000 genes as is commonly cited and attributed to the Nobel Laureate Walter Gilbert. The project also demonstrated how similar we all are. The DNA sequence between any two individuals is estimated to be 99.9% identical.[70,71]

Mapping of the human genome marks a new era in medical research, paving the way for the treatment and cure of many serious diseases. In the 21st century, we are witnessing an exciting new chapter being written in the history of diabetes. There is genuine hope in our search for a cure.

FIGURE 51
Decoding DNA. Limited
Edition First Day Cover.
Dr. Francis Crick. BS29
Scientists. In the upper
right-hand corner is a
U.K. Millennium 1999
stamp with three strands
of DNA.

References

1. Schuessler R: Stamping out diabetes. *Diabetes Forecast* 47(12):24–28, 1994
2. Papaspyros NS: *The History of Diabetes Mellitus*. 2nd ed. Stuttgart, Georg Thieme Verlag, 1964
3. Notelovitz M: Milestones in the history of diabetes—a brief survey. *South African Medical Journal* 44(40):1158–61, 1970
4. Osler W: *The Evolution of Modern Medicine*. New Haven, CT, Yale University Press, 1921
5. Lyons AS, Petrucelli R II: *Medicine An Illustrated History*. New York, Abradale Press, Harry N. Abrams, 1987
6. Chakravorty RC: Imhotep: the first physician. *Topical Time* 51(6):22–23, 2000
7. Bryan CP: *Ancient Egyptian Medicine The Papyrus Ebers*. Translated from the German version. Unchanged reprint of the Edition. London, Ares Publishers, 1930; Chicago, 1974
8. Gemmill CL: The Greek concept of diabetes. *Bulletin of the New York Academy of Medicine* 48(8):1033–36, 1972
9. Lloyd GER (Ed.): *Hippocratic Writings*. Harmondsworth, Middlesex, England, Pelican Books, 1978
10. Henshen F: On the term diabetes in the works of Areateus and Galen. *Medical History* 13(2):190–92, 1969
11. Maimonides M: *The Medical Aphorisms of Moses Maimonides*. Rosner F, Ed., translator. Haifa, Israel, Maimonides Research Institute, 1989
12. Major RH: *Classic Descriptions of Disease*. 3rd ed. Springfield, IL, Charles C. Thomas, 1945, p. 235–37
13. Reed JA: Aretaeus, the Cappadocian. *Diabetes* 46:419–21, 1954

14. Adams F (Ed., translator): The Extant Works of Aretaeus, the Cappadocian. London, The Sydenham Society, 1856, p. 338–40 (Courtesy of the Malloch Rare Book Room of the New York Academy of Medicine)

15. Abou-Aly A: *The Medical Writings of Rufus Ephesus.* PhD thesis. London, London University College, 1992

16. Frank LL: Diabetes mellitus in the texts of old Hindu medicine (Charaka, Susruta, Vagbhata). *American Journal of Gastroenterology* 27:76–95, 1957

17. Veith I (Ed., translator): *Huang Ti Nei Ching Su Wen: The Yellow Emperor's Classic of Internal Medicine.* Berkeley, University of California Press, 1966

18. Avicenna (Ibn Sina): *A Treatise on the Canon of Medicine, Incorporating a Translation of the First Book.* Gruner OC, Ed. London, Luzac & Co., 1930

19. Rosner F: Nephrology and urinalysis in the writings of Moses Maimonides. *American Journal of Kidney Diseases* 24(2):222–27, 1994

20. Paracelsus: Libri Secundi di Tartaro Tractus III. Cap. II De Diabetica. In *Dritter Theil Der Bücher und Schrifften des Edlen Hochgelehrten und Bewehrten Philosophi und Medici Philippi Theophrasti Bombast von Honheim Paracelsi gennant*, Frankfort, Wechels, 1603, p. 170. Cited by Major RH: *Classic Descriptions of Disease.* 3rd ed. Springfield, IL, Charles C. Thomas, 1945, p. 235–60

21. Cushing H: *A Bio-Bibliography of Andreas Vesalius.* 2nd ed. Hamden, CT, Archon Books, 1962

22. Norwich I: Andreas Vesalius: a bio-bibliographic study. *South African Medical Journal* 41(17):431–40, 1967

23. Vesalius A: *De Humanis Corporis Fabrica Libri Septem.* 2nd ed. Basel, Oporinus, 1555 (Courtesy of the New York Academy of Medicine)

24. Saunders JB deCM, O'Malley CD: *The Illustrations from the Works of Andreas Vesalius of Brussels.* New York, Gryphon Editions, The Classics Of Surgery Library, Special Edition, 1993

25. Harvey W: *Exercitatio Anatomica de Motu Cordis et Sanguinis in Animalibus: An Anatomical Study on the Motion of the Heart and Blood.* 3rd ed. Leake CD, Ed., translator. Springfield, IL, Charles C. Thomas, 1941

26. De Graaf R: *Tractatus Anatomico Medicus de Succi Pancreatici Natura & Usu.* Leyden, The Netherlands, 1671 (Courtesy of the New York Academy of Medicine)

27. Hughes JT: *Thomas Willis 1621–1675: His Life and Work.* Dorchester, Dorset, UK, Royal Society of Medicine Services Limited, Henry Ling Ltd. at the Dorset Press, 1991

28. Willis T: *Pharmaceutice Rationalis or an Exercitation of the Operations of Medicines in Human Bodies.* London, Dring, Harper and Leigh, 1679, p. 79. Cited by Major RH: *Classic Descriptions of Disease.* 3rd ed. Springfield, IL, Charles C. Thomas, 1945, p. 240–42

29. Dobson M: Experiments and observations on the urine in a diabetes. *Medical Observations and Inquiries* 5:298, 1776. Cited by Major RH: *Classic Descriptions of Disease.* 3rd ed. Springfield, IL, Charles C. Thomas, 1945, p. 242–45

30. Doig A, Ferguson JPS, Milne IA, Passmore R (Eds.): *William Cullen and the Eighteenth Century Medical World: A Bicentenary Exhibition and Symposium Arranged by the Royal College of Physicians of Edinburgh in 1990.* Edinburgh, Edinburgh University Press, 1993

31. Risse GB: "Doctor William Cullen, Physician, Edinburgh": a consultation practice in the eighteenth century. *Bulletin of the History of Medicine* 48:338–51, 1974

32. Cullen W: *Synopsis and Nosology, Being an Arrangement and Definition of Diseases.* First translation from Latin to English. Hartford, CT, Nathaniel Patten, 1792

33. Cullen W: Draft of letter from William Cullen to Matthew Dobson, re diabetes (Thompson I,625). c1775; Reference Code: GB 247 MS Cullen 137. Located at Department of Special Collections, Glasgow University Library, UK

34. Rollo J: *Cases of the Diabetes Mellitus; with the Results of the Trials of Certain Acids, and Other Substances in the Cure of the Lues Venerea.* 2nd ed. London, T. Gillet, for C. Dilly, In The Poultry, 1798

35. Levine R: Diabetes: the pancreas and insulin, a retrospective review. *Canadian Journal of Biochemistry* 57(6):447–54, 1979

36. Bliss M: *The Discovery of Insulin.* Chicago, University of Chicago Press, 1982

37. Rolleston HD: *The Endocrine Organs in Health and Disease.* London, Oxford University Press, 1936

38. Olmsted JMD, Olmsted EH: *Claude Bernard & the Experimental Method in Medicine.* New York, Henry Schuman, 1952, p. 49–108

39. Sakula A: Paul Langerhans (1847–1888): a centenary tribute. *Journal of the Royal Society of Medicine* 81:414–15, 1988

40. von Mering J, Minkowski O: Diabetes mellitus after extirpation of the pancreas. *Archiv fuer Experimentelle Pathologie und Pharmakologie* 26:375, 1889–90. Cited by Major RH: *Classic Descriptions of Disease.* 3rd ed. Springfield, IL, Charles C. Thomas, 1945, p. 250–53

41. Banting FG, Best CH: The discovery and preparation of insulin. *University of Toronto Medical Journal* 1:24-28, 1924

42. Opie EL: On the relation of the chronic interstitial pancreatitis to the islands of Langerhans and to diabetes mellitus. *Journal of Experimental Medicine* 5(4):419, 1901. Cited by Major RH: *Classic Descriptions of Disease.* 3rd ed. Springfield, IL, Charles C. Thomas, 1945, p. 254–56

43. Saffran M: Banting and Best and those who went before. *Hospital Practice* 123–32, 1992

44. Barron M: The relation of the islets of Langerhans to diabetes with special reference to cases of pancreatic lithiasis. *Journal of Surgery, Gynecology and Obstetrics* 31(5):437–48, 1920

45. Banting FG, Best CH: The internal secretion of the pancreas. *Journal of Laboratory and Clinical Medicine* 7:265, 1922

46. Banting FG, Best CH, Collip JB, Campbell WR, Fletcher AA: Pancreatic extracts in the treatment of diabetes mellitus. *Canadian Medical Association Journal* 2:141–46, 1922

47. Best CH: Fiftieth anniversary of insulin. *Modern Medicine of Canada* 26:7–9, 1971

48. Nobel e-Museum: Banting FG, Macleod JJR. The Nobel Prize in Medicine or Physiology 1923 "for the discovery of insulin." The Nobel Foundation. *http://www.nobel.se/medicine/laureates/1923/.* Accessed January 4, 1999

49. Teichman SL, Aldea PA: The other side of the insulin story: Paulescu's contribution. *New York State Journal of Medicine* 84(6):312–16, 1984

50. Teichman SL, Aldea PA: Nicolas Constantin Paulescu (1869–1931) discovered insulin before Banting and Best and inspired Harvey Cushing's work on the pituitary gland. *Revue Roumaine de Morphologie d'Embryologie et de Physiologie Physiologie* 22(2):121–34, 1985

51. Ionescu-Tirgoviste C: Insulin, the molecule of the century. *Archives of Physiology and Biochemistry* 104(7):807–13, 1996

52. Nobel e-Museum: Krogh SAS. The Nobel Prize in Medicine or Physiology 1920 "for his discovery of the capillary motor regulating mechanism." The Nobel Foundation. *http://www.nobel.se/medicine/laureates/1920/.* Accessed January 31, 2001

53. Novo Nordisk A/S: *Novo Nordisk History.* Denmark, Novo Nordisk A/S, January 1996

54. Murnaghan JH, Talalay P: John Jacob Abel and the crystallization of insulin. *Perspectives in Biology and Medicine* 10(3):334–80, 1967

55. Nobel e-Museum: Sanger F. The Nobel Prize in Chemistry 1958 "for his work on the structure of proteins, especially that of insulin." The Nobel Foundation. *http://www.nobel.se/chemistry/laureates/1958/.* Accessed February 11, 2001

56. Nobel e-Museum: Berg P, Gilbert W, Sanger F. The Nobel Prize in Chemistry 1980, "for his fundamental studies of the biochemistry of

nucleic acids, with particular regard to recombinant-DNA," and "for their contributions concerning the base sequences in nucleic acids." The Nobel Foundation. *http://www.nobel.se/chemistry/laureates/1980/*. Accessed February 11, 2001

57. Nobel e-Museum: Cori C, Cori G. The Nobel Prize in Medicine or Physiology 1947 "for their discovery of the catalytic conversion of glycogen." The Nobel Foundation. *http://www.nobel.se/medicine/laureates/1947/*. Accessed January 4, 1999

58. Garrison FH: *An Introduction to the History of Medicine.* 4th ed. Philadelphia, WB Saunders, 1929

59. Loubatières A: The discovery of hypoglycemic sulfonamides and particularly of their action mechanism. *Acta Diabetologia* 6(Suppl. 1): 20–56, 1969

60. Henquin J-C: The fiftieth anniversary of hypoglycemic sulphonamides: how did the mother compound work? *Diabetologia* 35:907–12, 1992

61. Nobel e-Museum: Yalow RS. The Nobel Prize in Medicine or Physiology 1977, "for the development of radioimmunoassays of peptide hormones." The Nobel Foundation. *http://www.nobel.se/medicine/laureates/1977/*. Accessed December 30, 2000

62. Yalow RS: Radioimmunoassay: A Probe For Fine Structure of Biologic Systems. Nobel Lecture, December 8, 1977, Stockholm, Sweden

63. Mendosa R: History of blood glucose meters: transcripts of the interviews. *http://www.mendosa.com*. Accessed February 2, 2001

64. The Diabetes Control and Complications Trial Research Group: The effect of intensive treatment of diabetes on the development and progression of long-term complications in insulin-dependent diabetes mellitus. *New England Journal of Medicine* 329:977–86, 1993

65. United Kingdom Prospective Diabetes Study Group: Intensive blood-glucose control with sulphonylureas or insulin compared with conventional treatment and risk of complications in patients with type 2 diabetes (UKPDS 33). *Lancet* 352:837–53, 1998

66. Joslin EP: The menace of diabetic gangrene. *New England Journal of Medicine* 211(1):16–20, 1934

67. Diabetes Research Working Group: *Conquering Diabetes: A Strategic Plan For The 21st Century.* Bethesda, MD, National Diabetes Information Clearinghouse, NDIC-DRWG, 1999

68. Watson J, Crick F: Molecular structure of nucleic acids: a structure for deoxyribose nucleic acid. *Nature* 171(4356):737–38, 1953

69. Nobel e-Museum: Crick FH, Watson JD, Wilkins MH. The Nobel Prize in Medicine or Physiology 1962, "for their discoveries concerning the molecular structure of nucleic acids and its significance for information

transfer in living material." The Nobel Foundation. *http://www.nobel. se/medicine/laureates/1962/*. Accessed February 17, 2001

70. Collins F, Mansoura MK: The human genome project. *Cancer* 91(Suppl. 1):221–25, 2001

71. Venter CJ, Adams MD, Myers EW, et al.: The sequence of the human genome. *Science* 291(5507):1304–51, 2001

Philatelic
References

Athale DM: Through the eyes of philately. *Scalpel & Tongs* May–June 1995

Chakravorty RC: Imhotep: the first physician. *Topical Time* 51(6):22–23, 2000

Chudley AE: Genetic landmarks through philately: a brief history of diabetes mellitus. *Clinical Genetics* 55:231–33, 1999

Furukawa A: *Medical History Through Postage Stamps*. St. Louis, Ishiyaku EuroAmerica, 1994

Onat T: The history of endocrinology in philately. *Journal of Pediatric Endocrinology and Metabolism* 10:371–77, 1997

O'Rahilly R: Philatelic introduction to the history of anatomy. *Clinical Anatomy* 10:337–40, 1997

Prout G: *The Nobel Prize in Physiology or Medicine 100 years (1901–2000): A Philatelic Odyssey by Gwen Prout, MD*. Canada, 2000

Schuessler R: Stamping out diabetes. *Diabetes Forecast* 47(12):24–28, 1994

Tan MH: Look closer. *Diabetes Forecast* 33(5):32–33, 1980

Tierney JT: Andreas Vesalius, anatomist of Padua. *Medicine and Health Rhode Island* 79(4):154, 1996

Wilson T: Imhotep to insulin on stamps: is there a doctor in your album? *Topical Time* 33(4):18–20, 1982

Glossary

diabetes insipidus: a disease resulting from lack of pituitary anti-diurectic hormone that mimics diabetes mellitus in causing the release of very large amounts of pale urine

diabetes mellitus: metabolic disease caused by the relative or absolute deficiency of insulin, resulting in body's inability to utilize carbohydrate, leading to high blood glucose levels

glycogenesis: action of glucose being stored as glycogen

glycosuria: high levels of glucose in the urine

hyperglycemia: abnormally high levels of glucose in the blood

hypoglycemia: abnormally low levels of glucose in the blood

ketoacidosis: acidic imbalance in body's fluids caused by lack of insulin

ketones: toxic acidic by-products of the burning of body fat for energy

polydipsia: excessive thirst

polyuria: excessive, frequent urination

Philatelic Resources

JOURNALS

Topical Time, *Journal of Thematic Philately*.
Published by the American Topical Association. Membership
information available at *http://home.prcn.org/~pauld/ata/*

Scalpel & Tongs, *American Journal of Medical Philately*.
Published by the Medical Subjects Unit of the American
Topical Association. Subscription information available at
http://home.prcn.org/~pauld/ata/units.htm

WEB SITES

American Philatelic Society:
http://americanphilatelic.org

American Topical Association:
http://home.prcn.org/~pauld/ata/

Biographies of People of the World:
http://www.philately.com/philately/biographies.htm

General philately:
http://www.philately.com

Joseph Luft's Philatelic Resources:
http://www.execpc.com/~joeluft/

Journal Club on the Web, physicians on stamps:
http://www.journalclub.org/stamps/

Linn's Stamp News, weekly stamp news:
http://www.linns.com/

Medi Theme:
http://www.philately.com/philately/medi_theme_v14_n4.htm

Stamp Link, links to philatelic sites:
http://www.stamplink.com/

Scott Publishing Co., stamp catalog:
http://www.scottonline.com

Stamp^2.com, philately and the stamp trade:
http://www.stamp2.com/

Stamp exchange:
http://www.stampfinder.com

Stamp search:
http://www.zillionsofstamps.com/

United States Postal Service philatelic news:
http://new.usps.com

Universal Postal Union (UPU), postal statistics:
http://www.upu.org

The History of Diabetes Philatelic Checklist

DIABETES-SPECIFIC SUBJECTS

(the stamp or subject is directly related to diabetes)

SUBJECT (SEE PAGE)	COUNTRY	ISSUED	SCOTT CATALOG #	DESCRIPTION
Aretaeus (9)	Transkei	1990	235	Aretaeus 130-200 A.D.
Banting & Best	Croatia	1996	RA 79	75th Anniversary of the Discovery of Insulin.
Banting & Best (42)	Kuwait	1971	523-524	Banting & Best 50th Anniv Discovery of Insulin 1921-1971.
Banting & Best (41)	Uruguay	1972	C385	50th Anniv Discovery of Insulin, WHO Emblem.
Banting, Frederick G. (39)	Canada	1971	533	Laboratory Equipment used for Insulin Discovery.
Banting, Frederick G. (42)	Canada	1991	1304	Sir Frederick G. Banting 1891-1941.
Banting, Frederick G. (37)	Canada	1999	1822a	Frederick Banting, Diabetes.
Banting, Frederick G. (40)	Transkei	1990	238	Frederick Banting 1891-1941.
Banting, Frederick G.	Switzerland	1971	539	Frederick G. Banting (1891-1941)
Banting, Frederick G.	Comoro Islands	1977	258	Nobel Prize, 75th anniversary. Banting and Nobel Prize Winners
Benedict's test (36)	Belgium	1971	811	Bendict's Test, Molecule of Proinsulin.
Bernard, Claude (32)	Transkei	1990	236	Claude Bernard (1813-1878).
Bernard, Claude	France	1978	B510	Claude Bernard (1813-1878).
Bernard, Claude	France	1939-40	B89, B89A	Claude Bernard (1813-1878).
Bernard, Claude	Argentina	1959	683	21st International Congress of Physiological Sciences, Buenos Aires.
Complications—amputation (65)	Dominican Republic	1974	725-726	Fight Against Diabetes 4c, Amputation.

The History of Diabetes Philatelic Checklist (*Continued*)

DIABETES-SPECIFIC SUBJECTS

(the stamp or subject is directly related to diabetes)

SUBJECT (SEE PAGE)	COUNTRY	ISSUED	SCOTT CATALOG #	DESCRIPTION
Complications—CVD (63)	Dominican Republic	1979	811	Dominican Instit. Cardiology. Heart, Diseased Blood Vessels.
Complications—eye (60)	Austria	1979	1130	Diseased Eye & Blood Vessels.
Complications—eye, heart (63)	Dominican Republic	1974	C219	Fight Against Diabetes 33c, Eye and Heart.
Complications—kidney (62)	Austria	1990	1515	Dialysis and Kidney Transplantation.
Complications—kidney (62)	Dominican Republic	1974	C218	Fight Against Diabetes 7c, Kidney.
Cori, Carl (50)	Gabon	1995	803a	Carl F. Cori, Nobel Prize Sheetlet III, Cori cycle.
Cori, Gerty (50)	Gabon	1995	803a	Gerty T. Cori, Nobel Prize Sheetlet III, Cori cycle.
Diabetes Awareness (59)	Brazil	1992	2380	National Diabetes Day.
Diabetes Awareness (58)	USA	2001	3503	Know More About Diabetes.
Diabetes Awareness	Dominican Republic	1989	1064	VII Latin American Congress of Diabetes.
Diabetes Awareness	Mexico	2000	2211	Federacion Internacional De Diabetes 1950-2000 Hummingbird.
Diabetes Education (58)	St. Vincent	1989	1305	25th Anniversary Lions International—Diabetes Education.
Ebers Papyrus (5)	Egypt	1971	864	Hesy Ra, Ebers Papyrus, WHO emblem.
Ebers Papyrus	German Democratic Republic	1991	2207	Papyrus Ebers.
Glucose Monitoring (55)	St. Vincent	1989	1306	25th Anniversary Lions International—Glucose monitoring.
Insulin	China	1976	1266	Scientific Research, 3-D structure of Insulin.

Name	Country	Year	Catalog	Description
Insulin Crystals (48)	Denmark	1990	B75	Insulin Crystals, Danish Diabetes Assoc 1940-1990.
Insulin Crystals (49)	Japan	1994	2433	Intl. Diabetes Federation, 15th Congress, Kobe.
Krogh, August Steenberg (47)	Sweden	1980	1342	Nobel Prize Winner 1920 August Krogh—Nordisk.
Minkowski, Oscar (35)	Transkei	1990	237	Oscar Minkowski 1858-1931.
Paulescu (43)	Romania	1994	3966	Nicholas C. Paulescu 1869-1931.
Sanger, Frederick	Palau	2000		Frederick Sanger, Nobel Prize in Chemistry
Yalow, Rosalyn (53)	Sierra Leone	1995	1844c	Rosalyn Sussman Yalow, Nobel Prize 1977, Radioimmunoassay (RIA)

The History of Diabetes Philatelic Checklist *(Continued)*

DIABETES-RELATED SUBJECTS

(the stamp or subject is connected to the history of diabetes)

SUBJECT (SEE PAGE)	COUNTRY	ISSUED	SCOTT CATALOG #	DESCRIPTION
Avicenna (14)	Iran	1954	B32, B31-35	Avicenna Ibn-Sina. Set of 5 stamps. Avicenna's Tomb at Hamadan.
Avicenna (15)	Austria	1982	1208	Urinalysis. Avicenna's Al-Qanun.
Avicenna	Hungary	1987	3061	Avicenna Ibn Szinna (980-1037).
DaVinci, Leonardo	France	1952	682	Leonardo DaVinci 1452-1519, 500th year of his birth.
DNA (back cover)	Israel	1988	980	Genetic Engineering. DNA Double Helix.
DNA—Crick (70)	United Kingdom	1999		FDC Decoding DNA, Francis Crick.
DNA—Watson, Crick, Wilkins (68)	Sweden	1989	1773	Watson, Crick & Wilkins, DNA dbl helix . Nobel Prize 1962.
DNA—Arber, Nathans, Smith (69)	Sweden	1989	1774	Arber, Nathans and Smith. Nobel Prize 1978.
Galen (8)	Hungary	1989	3213	Galen 120-201 A.D.
Galen	Yemen	1966		Galen. WHO New Headquarters Building. Yemen Arab Republic.
Harvey, William (22)	Russia	1957	1947	300th Anniversary of the Death of William Harvey, 1578-1657.
Harvey, William	Argentina	1959	682	21st International Congress of Physiological Sciences, Buenos Aires.
Harvey, William	Hungary	1987	3064	William Harvey (1578-1657), English physician, anatomist.
Heart (64)	Greece	1981	1396	Heart and Vessels, 15th Cardiovascular Surgery Conference.

Topic	Country	Year	Catalog	Description
Hindu Medicine (11)	Nepal	1977	337	Dhanvantari. Health Day.
Hindu Medicine—Ayurveda	Sri Lanka	1979	563	50th Anniversary for Ayurveda Medical Institute 1929-1979.
Hippocrates (6)	Greece	1979	1326	Statue of Hippocrates & his oath, memorial stamp Hippocratic Foundation.
Hippocrates	Australia	1968	441	Hippocrates & Hands Holding Hypodermic.
Hippocrates	Greece	1948	528	Statue of Hippocrates.
Hippocrates	Hungary	1987	3060	Hippocrates (460-377 B.C.), Greek physician.
Hippocrates	Yemen	1966		Hippocrates. WHO New Headquarters Building. Yemen Arab Republic.
Hippocrates & Avicenna	Syria	1965	C339	Hippocrates and Avicenna.
Huang Ti (12)	China	1983	1847-48	Tomb of the Yellow Emperor.
Imhotep (4)	Egypt	1928	153	Imhotep, 100th Anniv. Medical Dept. University of Cairo.
Imhotep	Egypt	1968	740, 741	Imhotep. WHO 20th Anniversary (1948-1968).
Imhotep	Egypt	1981	1168	Imhotep. 20th International Congress on Occupational Health.
Kidneys	Greece	1979	1390	Torso showing kidneys, 8th Intl. Nephrology Conference, Athens.
Laser (61)	Israel	1988	981	Medical Engineering.
Maimonides (16)	Israel	1953	74	Moses Maimonides, 7th Intl Congress of History & Science.
Maimonides	Spain	1967	1463	Moses Maimonides.
Maimonides	Sierre Leone	1986	743	Maimonides (1135-1204), medieval Judaic scholar.
Maimonides	Grenada	1970	401, 402a	Moses Maimonides and a biology student.
Microscope (34)	German Democratic Republic	1980	2126	Microscope Amici (Modena, 1845).

The History of Diabetes Philatelic Checklist (*Continued*)
DIABETES-RELATED SUBJECTS
(the stamp or subject is connected to the history of diabetes)

SUBJECT (SEE PAGE)	COUNTRY	ISSUED	SCOTT CATALOG #	DESCRIPTION
Paracelsus (20)	Hungary	1989	3214	Paracelsus 1493-1541.
Paracelsus	West Germany	1949	B311	Paracelsus
Pavlov	Hungary	1989	3217	I.P. Pavlov 1849-1936.
Red Cross (52)	France	1940	B102	French Red Cross. Nurse & Wounded Soldier.
Red Cross—pig (46)	Finland	1998	B260-262	Finland Red Cross, Pig.
Thoth (back cover)	Egypt	1925	105	Thoth, patron god of physicians. Intl Congress of Geography, Cairo 1925.
Thoth	Egypt	1958	459	Thoth. 50th Anniversary of Cairo University (1908-1958).
Vesalius (21)	Belgium	1964	606	Vesalius 1515-1564. Woodcut portrait 50c.
Vesalius	Belgium	1942	B320	Vesalius 1514-1564.

Index

P

Pancreas, illustration of, 23–24
Papaspyros, 10
Paracelsus, 17, 19–21, 88
Paulescu, Nicholas, 35, 41–43, 88
Pavlov, 88
Peripheral arterial disease, 63
Pharmacology, 48
Philatelic checklist, 83–88
Philately, xv
   medical, viii
Pig, 88
Polydipsia, 16, 79
Polyuria, 4, 16, 79
Prameha, 10–11
Preventive medicine, 7
Proinsulin, 49
Protein chemistry, 48

R

Radioimmunological Assay (RIA),
   53
Red Cross, 88
   pig, 88
Renaissance, 19–30
Retinopathy, 59, 61
Rollo, John, 28–30
Rufus of Ephesus, 10

S

Sanders, Lee, viii–ix, xi–xii
Sanger, Frederick, 32, 48–50, 85
Schally, Andrew, 53
Schuessler, Raymond, xv
Scott, E.L., 35, 41
Self-management of blood glucose
   (SMBG), 54
Sharpy-Schafer, Sir Edward Albert,
   36
Smith, H.O., 68, 86

Steiner, Donald, 49
Stroke, 63
Sulfonamides, 51–52
Susruta, 10–12

T

T cell–mediated autoimmune dis-
   ease, 67
Thoth, 3–4, 88
Topical Time, ATA's *Journal of The-
   matic Philately*, xvi, 81
Treatments for diabetes, 2, 5, 29

U

Unger, G., 45
United Kingdom Prospective
   Diabetes Study (UKPDS),
   60–61
Universal Postal Union, vii

V

Vagbhata, 10
Vedic scriptures, 10
Vesalius, Andreas, 19, 21–22, 88
Von Mering, Joseph, 34–35

W

Watson, James D., 67–68, 86
Wilkins, Maurice H.F., 68, 86
Willis, Thomas, 24–26
World Health Day, 5, 41
World Health Organization, 5, 8,
   41–42

Y

Yalow, Rosalyn Sussman, 32,
   52–54, 85
Yellow Emperor, 12

Z

Zuelzer, Georg Ludwig, 35

About the American Diabetes Association

The American Diabetes Association is the nation's leading voluntary health organization supporting diabetes research, information, and advocacy. Its mission is to prevent and cure diabetes and to improve the lives of all people affected by diabetes. The American Diabetes Association is the leading publisher of comprehensive diabetes information. Its huge library of practical and authoritative books for people with diabetes covers every aspect of self-care—cooking and nutrition, fitness, weight control, medications, complications, emotional issues, and general self-care.

To order American Diabetes Association books: Call 1-800-232-6733. http://store.diabetes.org [Note: there is no need to use **www** when typing this particular Web address]

To join the American Diabetes Association: Call 1-800-806-7801. www.diabetes.org/membership

For more information about diabetes or ADA programs and services: Call 1-800-342-2383. E-mail: Customerservice@diabetes.org.www.diabetes.org

To locate an ADA/NCQA Recognized Provider of quality diabetes care in your area: Call 1-703-549-1500 ext. 2202. www.diabetes.org/recognition/Physicians/ListAll.asp

To find an ADA Recognized Education Program in your area: Call 1-888-232-0822. www.diabetes.org/recognition/education.asp

To join the fight to increase funding for diabetes research, end discrimination, and improve insurance coverage: Call 1-800-342-2383. www.diabetes.org/advocacy

To find out how you can get involved with the programs in your community: Call 1-800-342-2383. See below for program Web addresses.

- *American Diabetes Month:* Educational activities aimed at those diagnosed with diabetes—month of November. www.diabetes.org/ADM
- *American Diabetes Alert:* Annual public awareness campaign to find the undiagnosed—held the fourth Tuesday in March. www.diabetes.org/alert
- *The Diabetes Assistance & Resources Program (DAR):* Diabetes awareness program targeted to the Latino community. www.diabetes.org/DAR
- *African American Program:* Diabetes awareness program targeted to the African American community. www.diabetes.org/africanamerican
- *Awakening the Spirit: Pathways to Diabetes Prevention & Control:* Diabetes awareness program targeted to the Native American community. www.diabetes.org/awakening

To obtain information on making a planned gift or charitable bequest: Call 1-888-700-7029. www.diabetes.org/ada/plan.asp

To make a donation or memorial contribution: Call 1-800-342-2383. www.diabetes.org/ada/cont.asp